make your group
grow

"Josh Hunt believes in the power of small-group ministry—and his belief is contagious. In his new book, *Make Your Group Grow*, Josh presents sound application to easy-to-understand research that will benefit every size and style of church. Your groups and leadership will benefit from this book."

—Ed Stetzer
Author and church planter

"Josh has written a book that is clear, simple, and a proven path for growing your small-group ministry. I loved reading it. I wrote notes in the margin as I thought about what we're doing right and what we need to improve. I highly encourage every pastor and church leader to read this book. I want all of our small-group leaders to have a copy. It's one of the best things I've read on groups. Instead of focusing on a single model, Josh deals with things *every* model has to have."

—Bob Roberts
Pastor and author, *The Multiplying Church*

"Books on small groups abound, but few writers have produced studies based on surveys of small-group leaders. If you're looking for a book filled with empirical evidence, practical suggestions, and numerous examples from real churches, this is the book for you."

—Chuck Lawless
Dean, Billy Graham School of Missions and Evangelism

"I love this book! *Make Your Group Grow* is an extraordinarily helpful book for teachers and leaders of both Sunday schools and small groups. It's filled with practical advice and real-world examples. You'll fly through this book, then revisit it over and over to pick up new tips that lead to healthy, growing groups. In an era of complexity, Josh reaffirms the simple core of great groups and classes."

—Bill Search
Pastor and author, *Simple Small Groups*

"Exposing methodological myths, unearthing what must be done and how to do it in this era, and inspiring latent leaders are the keys to an astoundingly effective and growing Sunday school. Josh not only does all of these things, but courageously sets a new standard for the local church's most vital ministry—its groups."

—Rick Howerton
Trainer and "small group-ologist"

"Josh Hunt delivers...again! *Make Your Group Grow* is built on the research and responses of actual teachers and actual Sunday school classes. The book is more than what someone thinks might make a Sunday school grow. Josh dissects actual classes and examines the heart of what does and doesn't make a difference in helping them grow. Once in a while a book comes along that every Sunday school leader should read. *Make Your Group Grow* is one of those books."

—Dr. Steve R. Parr
Author, *Sunday School That Really Works*

make your group
grow
by josh hunt

simple stuff that really works

Group
Loveland, Colorado
group.com

Group resources actually work!

This Group resource incorporates our R.E.A.L. approach to ministry. It reinforces a growing friendship with Jesus, encourages long-term learning, and results in life transformation, because it's

Relational
Learner-to-learner interaction enhances learning and builds Christian friendships.

Experiential
What learners experience through discussion and action sticks with them up to 9 times longer than what they simply hear or read.

Applicable
The aim of Christian education is to equip learners to be both hearers and doers of God's Word.

Learner-based
Learners understand and retain more when the learning process takes into consideration how they learn best.

make your group
grow simple stuff that really works
by josh hunt

Visit our website: **group.com**

Credits
Editor: Carl Simmons
Chief Creative Officer: Joani Schultz
Executive Editor: Becki Manni
Art Director: Paul Povolni
Cover Designer: Rebecca Parrott

Book Designer: Jean Bruns
Graph Designer: Kristy Lehman
Typesetting: Paragon Prepress
Production Manager: DeAnne Lear

ISBN 978-0-7644-4015-1

10 9 8 7 6 5 4 3 2 1   19 18 17 16 15 14 13 12 11 10

Printed in the United States of America.

contents

make your group
grow

introduction

more than 12 years ago, I wrote a book titled *You Can Double Your Class in Two Years or Less* (Group). It was based on my own experiences at growing groups and my local church. Our church had grown from one service and one Bible study hour to four services and four Bible study hours, and I believed the principles we used could be broadly applied to grow almost any church.

The book launched me into a speaking and training career that has taken me all around the world. I conduct about 100 conferences a year at local churches and denominational meetings, and to date I've logged 1.8 million miles on American Airlines alone. Host churches routinely report positive feedback from the conferences and positive results afterward.

Still, I secretly wondered sometimes, as I flew home on late-night flights, if what I was teaching was really working.

Life as a full-time trainer/speaker is different from local church work. In a way, it's exciting because I feel like I'm impacting lots of churches. Nonetheless, I'm not there to see the results, so I always wonder how much impact I'm actually having. Are people putting these principles into practice? Are the principles working? Are the churches getting the same results I got?

The principles of *You Can Double Your Class in Two Years or Less* are simple. (The best ideas always are, aren't they?) I used the acronym TIGER to communicate them:

Teach a halfway decent lesson each and every week; nothing less will do. You don't have to be Zig Ziglar or Beth Moore or Elmer Towns to grow a group, but you *do* need to be committed to teaching an engaging, application-rich, and biblically solid lesson.

Invite every member and every potential member to every fellowship every month. That's a lot of *every*s. But it's not difficult to do if you're committed to it. I teach a party-driven strategy that's both relational and intentional.

Give Friday nights to Jesus. Mind you, it doesn't *have* to be a Friday night. The real idea here is this: In addition to consistently inviting every member and every potential member to larger events, invite people to smaller, more informal events, as well. Have friends over on a Friday night for games and dessert, and make sure you invite others from outside the group.

Encourage the group toward ministry, whether inside or outside the group. Twelve years on the road have taught me that group leaders tend to not be the most fun people in our churches. They like to study and read and prepare and present. They're not much for parties. Therefore, they need a team of people to help them. They need inreach leaders and outreach leaders and fellowship leaders. They need to equip others so they can reach others for Jesus as a team.

Reproduce your group. By definition, if a group grows, it can't *stay* a small group. Eventually you need to start new groups. Doubling a group is not so much about going from 10 to 20 as it is about going from one group to two. This can be done in a variety of ways; some ways are more disruptive than others. We'll talk more about that later.

The results of doubling groups are amazing. If you want to know where your group could be in five years, and you're on pace to double every 18 months, just add a zero every five years. If a group of 10 doubled every 18 months, it would reach 1,000 people for God in 10 years. If the group continued to grow at that pace, it would reach the entire world population in about 43 years. *One group that continued to double would fulfill the Great Commission.* I hope that idea gets you as excited as it gets me. That's how important this is.

So night after night, week after week, for the last 12 years, I've pounded away on these five principles. But again, secretly, I've wondered if they really work.

So I asked.

Let's do a survey (and another...)

During the past 50 years, there's been a lot of research on what makes the church grow at a congregational level. What we now need more of is research on what it takes to grow the church at the *micro*-church level. Hopefully others will build on the research done here.

I surveyed more than 1,000 teachers—many of whom have attended my seminars or visited my web page, joshhunt.com—to discover if what I was teaching was really working. I was looking for answers to questions including the following:

- Are groups that host lots of parties more likely to be growing than those that don't?
- Are groups that have a large team—lots of people helping—more likely to be growing?
- Are groups with "five-star" teachers—in terms of their teaching ability—significantly more likely to have growing groups than those with three- and four-star teachers? Is halfway decent *really* good enough?

In each case, I separated responses into the high and the low. If there were five possible answers, I threw out the middle ones and compared the top group with the bottom group. I wanted to see as much contrast as possible. I then divided my findings into four categories:

- Things that hardly mattered at all (less than 10 percent difference in likelihood of growth between the bottom and top groups)

- Things that mattered a little (11 to 100 percent more likelihood of growth in the top groups when compared with the bottom groups)
- Things that mattered a lot (Churches in the top group were more than twice as likely to be growing compared to churches in the bottom group, with a difference in likelihood from 101 to 1,000 percent.)
- The one thing that matters most (If your group is doing it, you're almost 11 times more likely to be growing than a group that isn't doing it.)

Short answer: This survey produced substantial confirmation that what I've been teaching over the past 12 years really works. But there were also some surprises. Some things that I said mattered a lot didn't matter much at all. And again, we'll look at all of this shortly.

What's more, this survey raised as many questions as it answered. Which led to another survey. Then another. And…well, you get the idea. This book brings the collective findings of those surveys together in one place. But there's way more to this book than stats.

Do you *really* like reading surveys?

I don't. Survey books make me tired. All those numbers make my eyes glaze over. I want this book to be more than numbers, or even how to make those numbers grow. Happily, I have another information source that may be more powerful than all the surveys put together—success stories.

I've heard hundreds of stories from group leaders who have doubled their groups every two years or less. I've videotaped many of those stories. I've shared meals with these leaders, been in their homes, exchanged e-mails, and visited with them on Facebook. I've seen them in action and seen God at work in them. And their groups are growing, in every sense of the word.

What's the big deal about numerical growth?

Occasionally I'm asked, "Does God *really* care about numbers?" Rather than give a theological answer, I'll allow the data to speak for itself. Growing groups tend to be better groups in every way. For example, growing groups are 59 percent more likely to report high levels of spiritual vibrancy. I'll define spiritual vibrancy in more detail in Chapter 6, but for now, what it means is that groups of people who love living the Christian life grow. And why *wouldn't* they?

Another question I'm sometimes asked is, "These growing groups—are they really reaching non-Christians, or are they just reaching the already convinced?" We now have the data. Growing groups reported being 65 percent more likely to have seen at least one person come to faith in Christ in the past year.

Do you need more workers in your church? Growing groups can help you there as well. Growing groups are nearly twice as likely to have sent out at least one worker.

One more. You'd like your people to feel loved, wouldn't you? That's more likely to happen in a growing group, too. In fact, members of groups that were not growing were *333 percent more likely* to report feeling *un*loved, when compared to members of growing groups.

In every way that I could find, growing groups are not just growing numerically. Growing groups almost always *are* better groups. I couldn't find an exception. I couldn't find one desirable behavior or characteristic that was more common with groups that were not growing. If you want better groups, you also want growing groups.

If you're a group leader, I hope you're now asking, "How can my group grow?" And if you're a pastor, you might be thinking, "How can *all* my church's groups grow?" Now we know. We can predict, with a high degree of accuracy, what will produce growth in a group, whether it's in a small-group or Sunday-school environment.

I'm confident that if you prayerfully follow the principles that have been affirmed or uncovered in these surveys, and in the personal accounts you'll find throughout this book, your groups will grow and make an impact for the kingdom of God such as you've only dreamed about until now.

So let's begin.

what makes groups grow— a bit

○ MAKE YOUR GROUP GROW

chapter 1

three things that matter a little

before we begin looking at the survey results, allow me to say something: I don't like some of the answers I got. I especially don't like some of the answers in this opening section. In fact, in some cases, I've taught exactly the opposite of what this survey reveals.

So let me go ahead and say this, too: I disagree with some of these findings. However, the facts are the facts; therefore, I'm going to report them just as they are. If you disagree with them, don't shoot me. I'm only the messenger.

On the other hand, don't disagree with me simply because you don't want to hear it. I didn't want to hear some of these things either. Instead, consider what God might be trying to show you. I'll bet you're already do-ing a *lot* of things right. But tweaking one or two small things may make all the difference.

Sixty years ago, longtime missionary Donald McGavran noticed some-thing when he returned to the United States. Two churches, sitting side by side, using similar programs with similarly trained pastors, were get-ting entirely different results. One was growing rapidly while the other was floundering. They both preached the good news of Jesus. They both believed the same things. But the outcomes were completely different. McGavran studied this principle and reported his findings in the seminal work *Understanding Church Growth*. This discovery began a surge of research on what makes churches grow and led to what is commonly known today as the church-growth movement.

I have witnessed this phenomenon myself: Two classes or groups in the same church, using the same literature with similarly trained leaders, will teach the same message and get entirely different results. One will grow and develop leaders and start new classes while the other flounders. We need to discover why. I hope my research described here leads to many more studies about what it takes to make a *group* grow.

But first, let's look at what usually doesn't work so well. Here are three things that, according to my research, mattered only a little in terms of their contribution to the growth of a group.

Who gets more of your time—outsiders or insiders?

I asked leaders who they spent more social time with—people inside the group or those outside it. I would have thought that spending more time with people outside the group would be a predictor of whether the group was growing. It would stand to reason that if a teacher spends significantly more time with people outside the group, those people will be more likely to come to the group.

Turns out I was wrong. Groups with leaders who spent 80 percent or more of their social time with people outside the group were 10 percent *less* likely to be growing than those whose leaders spent 80 percent or more of their time with those inside the group.

My take on these findings is that if you ignore the people in your group, it won't grow, no matter how much time you spend trying to get outsiders to join it. A leader spending most of his or her time with those outside the group rather than with those already in the group is analogous to a business spending all its money on advertising to the exclusion of product development.

The real winners were groups with leaders who balanced their time. Those in the middle (groups whose leaders spent no more than 60 percent of their time with outsiders or insiders) were 21 percent more likely to be growing than those whose leaders spent 80 percent or more of their time with people inside the class, and 33 percent more likely to be growing than those whose leaders spent 80 percent or more of their time with outsiders.

Balance. In all things. Jesus taught us to walk the narrow way. It's narrow because it's easy to fall into one extreme or the other. We need to care for people both outside and inside the group.

If you want to grow your group, try to balance the time you spend with people inside the class with the time you spend ministering to people on the outside.

Do groups have to catch the vision first?

I taught for several years that if we are going to see a doubling-group movement in our country, the groups themselves must embrace the vision of growing and dividing. After all, a group of 10 that doubles every 18 months can reach 1,000 people in 10 years, and a group of 10 that doubles every 18 months would reach *the whole world* in approximately 43 years. (Yes, I *do* say this a lot.) What an incredible opportunity!

So, why isn't it happening? My initial conclusion was that it's not happening because we don't *want* it to happen. The group has to first embrace the vision.

I had good reason to think this. Over the years, I've heard *lots* of people say, "But we don't want to double our class. Our class is comfortable the way we are." I assumed that growing groups were made up of a different breed of people—people who were fired up about the vision. With these racehorses, we could grow using any method or no method. I reasoned that groups that were growing *must* be comprised of people who really embraced the vision of doubling groups.

Not so. There was almost no difference (2 percent) in the likelihood of growth between those in the top and those in the bottom of this scale. I was shocked. People who really embraced the vision were only slightly more likely to be in groups that were doubling than those who didn't embrace the vision.

How can we explain this? Here's my attempt.

Imagine you're rocking along, facilitating a group, but not overtly pushing it to grow and multiply. How aware are you of your group's feelings about growing and multiplying? How likely would you be to report that your group is strongly opposed to the idea? Not so much, right?

Now, suppose you get bitten by the group-multiplication bug. You start actively talking to your group about growing and multiplying. What kind of response do you expect to get?

In case you're not sure, trust me—it's highly unlikely that your group will openly embrace the idea. You start ranting and raving about growing and dividing, and they'll start recoiling and resisting. How aware are you *now* of your group's feelings about the vision? How likely are you to report that your group is strongly opposed to growing and multiplying? *Very* likely.

The more the leader embraces the vision of growing and multiplying, the more likely he or she is to be aware of the group's resistance. Eventually, as the leader succeeds in growing and multiplying the group, more people get on board with the vision. But it takes time.

In short, I still believe that if a group has embraced the vision, it is more likely to be growing. Conversely, though, the more the vision is cast, the more aware the leader is of resistance. These factors offset each other, I think. But the facts remain the facts.

The lesson we *can* take away is this: If you want to grow your group and birth new groups, *you don't have to wait for your group to catch the vision.* Sometimes they've already embraced the vision and sometimes they haven't. Either way, groups usually only embrace the vision *after* they've seen it work a couple of times.

After a conference in the Houston area, a man come up to me with this testimony: "I bought your book [*You Can Double Your Class in Two Years or Less*], read it, and put it into practice. Our group grew. I presented the idea of multiplying. They hated it! They hated me! They hated *you*, Josh! But we did it anyway. Attendance actually dropped for a while. But we rocked along. We kept doing the things that had caused us to grow—

having parties and inviting every member and every potential member. We had the group well organized and lots of people were involved. A year went by. I looked up and noticed we had as many as we had before we divided. The other group was doing just about as well. I realized we would never have gotten that many to come to our small group. So, we divided again. People were grumpy, but not as grumpy as before because they had seen some positive results. We grew again and recently divided again. I'm starting to think I can do this!"

Most people catch a vision *after* they see results. It's much the same in other areas of life. You don't have to be *excited* about grilled chicken, broccoli, and exercise to lose weight; you just have to eat broccoli and grilled chicken—and, of course, exercise.

Lesson: Don't wait for your group to embrace the vision of growing and multiplying; just work the plan.

Does being a good organizer help?

Not as much as you'd think. Leaders who described themselves as having high organizational ability were only 7 percent more likely to be growing their groups, compared to those that described themselves as having low organizational ability.

What does matter, as we'll see later, is having a big team—getting lots of people engaged and helping. But how do you get lots of people helping if you're not good at organizing them?

The short answer: *You* don't.

A senior women's group had a good leader who was excellent at ministering to the many needs of the women in the class. However, the leader's husband became sick, and she was spending so much time caring for him that she could no longer lead the group.

Another woman stepped up to run the group. She was an excellent teacher who had been the main sub, and she did a great job of teaching. But this leader understood group life. She knew what needed to happen if the group were to function in a healthy way. And she knew she didn't have time to do it.

One day, she went to the group and said, "Let's make a deal. I'll prepare an interesting, biblical, helpful lesson each week. But you guys need to take care of everything else—all the parties, invitations, phone calls, meals, visits, and everything else. I'll take care of the teaching."

The group agreed, and then the group members did one more thing that was really key—they appointed one person to be the group coordinator. The coordinator got everybody else doing what needed to be done.

I once heard Bill Hybels say it this way: "What a wonderful plan God has for us: Let the teachers teach; let the leaders lead; let the mercy-givers give mercy." You don't have to be an organizational genius to grow a class. You do need to have a team of people helping you. And one person on that team needs to have the organizational skill to get everyone else doing what needs to be done.

So far, we've looked at three issues that matter only a little:

- Is it more important to spend time with insiders or outsiders? My discovery: Balanced is best.
- Does the group need to share your vision of growing and multiplying? My discovery: Don't wait until your group likes the idea; in fact, they probably *won't* like it at first. Just work the plan.
- Does being a good organizer mean your group will grow? My discovery: It will help, but not a ton. And that organizer doesn't have to be you. If you're not well organized, find someone in your group who is.

Let's move on to things that mattered…some.

four things that matter ...some

a s I've mentioned, I travel quite a bit. In fact, I once told my brother-in-law that I was in the top tier of American Airlines fliers—Executive Platinum—and that he should set that as a goal for himself. (He travels a bit for his job, too.) He responded that becoming Executive Platinum was an "anti-goal" for him—something he didn't care about achieving.

In a way, the things we've looked at so far are "anti-goals"—things we don't need to concentrate too much time and attention on. So now we move from things that don't matter much to things that do matter—some. Groups that do the following are 11 to 100 percent more likely to grow. So while there's even bigger fish to fry, four issues are worth paying attention to.

1. Should more time be spent on the class or the lesson?

I had my guess about which matters more. And I was right. But I thought it would matter a lot more than it does.

A Sunday school teacher or group leader may be very different from our idea of a traditional teacher and may, in fact, be more like a parent.

Paul spoke of this idea: "We were like a mother feeding and caring for her own children. We loved you so much that we shared with you not only God's Good News but our own lives, too...And you know that we treated each of you as a father treats his own children" (1 Thessalonians 2:7-8, 11).

Likewise, Jesus' plan for making disciples had a lot to do with spending time—lots of time—with those disciples. "He appointed twelve—designating them apostles—that they might be with him and that he might send them out to preach" (Mark 3:14, NIV).

For these reasons, I predicted that groups with leaders who focused primarily on their group members would be growing—and that, in contrast, groups with leaders who spent lots of time on the lesson would not.

As it turns out, spending more time with group members *is* a predictor of growth. Groups with leaders who spend more time with group members are 34 percent more likely to be growing than those with leaders who spend more time on the lesson.

So, it *does* make a difference. But compared to all the other factors we still have to look at, it's a comparatively small difference.

I have an educated guess as to why the gap isn't bigger. People who spend more time on the lesson are more likely to be better teachers. In fact, teachers who spend more time on the lesson are more likely to report that they are four- or five-star teachers. And people like to hear good teaching.

This suggests that there's more than one way to slice the pie. Spending time with your group members socially is the more effective route to growing your groups, but giving your time and attention to them through teaching also shows that you care about the people in your group—and that will shine through. People will usually forgive your lack of social skills if they can see that you really care about them. But spending time with your group members conveys that message more directly—and thus is more effective.

We'll get more into the value of good teaching in terms of growing your groups later in this chapter. Lucky the man or woman who has both strong teaching skills *and* strong people skills—and luckier the group who has him or her for a leader. And if you're truly bad enough at either one, you *will* struggle. Therefore, shore up your weaknesses. Make sure you're at least halfway decent at both. Then lean into your strengths.

Be careful, though, not to spend too much time on your weaknesses. It's an easy trap to fall into. For example, 77 percent of Americans believe that a student's *lowest* grades deserve the most attention.[1] If little Johnny comes home from school with one A, three Bs, and one C, most parents want to talk about the C. Strengths research done by the Gallup organization suggests that what they *ought* to be talking about is how to lean into the A subject. "Even the legendary Michael Jordan, who embodied the power of raw talent on the basketball court, could not become, well, the 'Michael Jordan' of golf or baseball, no matter how hard he tried."[2]

Likewise, over the past decade, Gallup surveyed more than 10 million people worldwide on the topic of employee engagement (how positive and productive they are at work). People working in fields that use their strengths are six times more likely to be engaged in their jobs and three times more likely to have an excellent quality of life in general.[3]

Again, we do need to shore up our weaknesses. If we're bad enough in critical areas, we're in trouble. If a kid is bad at math and incredible at English, we need to get that kid good enough at math to function in society. But we shouldn't try to make that student brilliant in math—everyone will get frustrated trying.

To recap, you can grow a group either through strong people skills or through strong teaching skills, but strong people skills are the easier route. Shore up whatever weaknesses you have, and lean into your strengths.

2. What should groups major in—outreach or spiritual growth?

This question is really a false dilemma. And I'll talk about why shortly. But first, let's look at the data.

Groups that saw their primary purpose as being more about reaching others outside the group than growing spiritually were 53 percent more likely to be growing than those groups that saw their primary purpose as growing spiritually.

This didn't come as a big surprise to me. Groups that see their primary purpose as reaching out *are* reaching out. *And* growing.

After seeing these results, though, I began to wonder about something else. Were groups who focused on reaching out in fact also more spiritually vibrant than those more inwardly focused groups? After all, you'd think that groups that focused on growing spiritually would also be more likely to report higher levels of spiritual vibrancy. I had certainly thought so until that very moment.

So I probed the data further. Sure enough, I had been wrong. Groups that saw their purpose as primarily about reaching out to others were exactly *twice as likely* to report the highest levels of spiritual vibrancy, compared with those that saw their primary purpose as spiritual growth.

The truth is, you can't grow close to God without caring about what God cares about. Here's a Bible trivia question for you: What's the context of the phrase, "And surely I am with you always"?

It's the Great Commission. Jesus taught that as we engage on mission with God in the task of advancing the kingdom, pushing back the darkness, we're going to experience a closeness to God that no Bible study can ever produce. (Please don't think I'm anti-Bible study; I think my life proves otherwise.)

Many have experienced this phenomenon in the context of a mission trip. There was something that happened that went beyond the excitement of jet travel. God was there. And as we engage in a lifetime mission with God to fulfill the Great Commission, Jesus will be with us. Always.

This is one of the many things I love about speaking and writing and serving God. I feel close to God when I serve. You will, too. If you're reading this book (and you are), you've no doubt already experienced this. You were teaching children, organizing a ministry project, making a phone call to encourage a friend, making a hospital visit, or doing any number of things that might relate to your gifting and calling. All of a sudden, there was this sense that you were in the flow of God's Spirit. God was there, and his presence was powerful.

This is life at its best, but I didn't always see it that way. Culture tends to give us the idea that life at its best is about leisure and relaxation, entertainment and excitement, or possessions and position. We don't naturally suppose that *our* lives, at their best, are about… serving *others*.

We used to sing a traditional song that went like this:

Praise Him! Praise Him!
Praise Him in the morning,
Praise Him at the noontime.
Praise Him! Praise Him!
Praise Him when the sun goes down.

I'd smile and sing. I enjoyed that little chorus. Then came the second verse:

Thank Him! Thank Him!
Thank Him in the morning,
Thank Him at the noontime.
Thank Him! Thank Him!
Thank Him when the sun goes down.

So far it's all good. I'm still smiling and singing.

Then the third verse would hit. I hated the third verse. I always hoped we wouldn't sing the third verse.

Serve Him! Serve Him!
Serve Him in the morning,
Serve Him at the noontime.
Serve Him! Serve Him!
Serve Him when the sun goes down.

I hated that verse because culture had taught me that life at its best was about leisure and entertainment and *stuff*. It was not about serving.

Forty years of serving God have taught me the opposite. Life at its best is about serving God the way he built you to serve. And for those in a group, life at its best is about serving God together—each one using the gifts that God has given him or her to serve God in pushing back the darkness and letting our light shine.

This is what's wrong with the sit-and-soak group. When members of a group want to "just get closer and closer to God" but don't care one whit about bringing others closer to God, they can't get close to God themselves. God is always on mission. Henry Blackaby taught us that if we want to get near to God, we must join God in what God is doing. And God is moving. Therefore, if we want to stay near to God, we must stay moving.

Jesus said, "My Father is always working" (John 5:17). God is always working. He is moving. He is like the wind. If we would draw near to God, we must keep up with him. There is a time to be still and know that he is God. But there's also a time to get off the Mount of Transfiguration and get down in the valley where the people are. God is moving. We must be moving as well. We must join God in what God is doing.

A group that is on mission with God in growing and reaching is not only more effective in growing and reaching, but also more effective at getting people closer to God—including themselves. If you want to increase the spiritual depth of your group, engage them on mission in serving God and reaching out beyond the confines of your group.

3. How important is a good teacher?

Leaders who describe themselves as four- or five-star teachers are 68 percent more likely to report that their groups are growing than those who describe themselves as one- or two-star teachers.

This one didn't surprise me. I would have predicted that the better the teaching, the more likely the growth. By level of self-description, it broke down like this:

- Five-star teachers—48 percent reported their groups were growing
- Four-star teachers—47 percent growing
- Three-star teachers—37 percent growing
- Two-star teachers—35 percent growing
- One-star teachers—6 percent growing

This puts to rest another myth you sometimes hear: "We're not growing numerically; I just concentrate on quality teaching." Maybe. But the opposite is much more likely to be true. The better the teaching, the more likely the growth. The less growth, the more likely that the teaching isn't that good either.

Part of how teachers rated themselves probably has to do with confidence. Confident teachers would naturally describe themselves as four- and five-star teachers more often than less confident teachers. But this is not just bravado. In a follow-up survey of participants, members of growing groups were 76 percent more likely to describe their teachers as five-star teachers and 27 percent more likely to describe their teachers as four-star teachers. Teachers of growing groups are more likely to describe themselves as better teachers—and their group members are more likely to describe them that way, too.

4. Does visitation still work?

Regular participation in visitation was a strong positive predictor of growth. Leaders who regularly visit those outside the church—whether that's follow-ups with visitors or absentees or even door-to-door visitation—are 78 percent more likely to have groups that are growing, compared with those who never or almost never pound the pavement.

There's a lesson in this finding that you won't read in a lot of church-growth books today. Try this: Stop by your average Christian bookstore. Go to the section for pastors and leaders, and peruse some of the titles. Chances are you'll come away with the idea that you have to be innovative, missional, purpose-driven, hip or cool or with-it or different to grow a church. If you're a pastor, you might think, "My church is never going to be any of those things. Can we still be effective? Can a 'normal' (and a bit old-fashioned) church like ours still be effective and useful to God in today's world?"

Yes!

I have a friend who's a pastor in El Paso, Texas. He has enjoyed remarkable growth in his church, doubling twice in about five years. I asked him how he did it. Because I've been to many church-growth conferences and read more than my share of current church-growth books, I poked him a bit, asking specific questions about his ministry.

"Do you have a hot band?" I probed.

"What?" He acted like he didn't understand the question, so I asked again.

"No, we don't have a hot band. Our music is completely traditional." Now, there's language you don't hear much anymore. Almost everyone describes the music as "blended," "contemporary," or in a few cases, "edgy." My friend used the word without apology. "Our music is completely traditional." But he didn't stop there. "Yeah, it's not only traditional; it's *bad* traditional."

"*Bad* traditional?"

"Yeah, bad, like *bad*. The piano isn't in tune, and the people don't play very well. The singers don't sing very well. Nothing is done very well. It's *bad*."

"How in the world did you double your church, then?"

"Well, here's how I did it. On day one, I went to work. I showed up at my office at 9:00 a.m., set down my keys, and walked right back out the front door to the house next door. I knocked on the door, and no one was home. I went to the next door. No one was home. I went to the next door. An elderly gentleman answers the door. I introduced myself. 'I'm Pastor Jim from the church next door. I just wanted to stop by and introduce myself and...' About this time he slammed the door in my face."

My friend said he went to the next house and the next and the next. Many people weren't home, but he kept notes so he could go back. A few people were rude. Many didn't seem interested. Then at house number 30, my friend got a better response. The woman there asked if my friend could go by and see her mom, who was in the hospital. He did. One thing led to another, and they later started coming to church.

"Around house number 50," he said, "I really hit the jackpot. The people I met at this point were totally interested. I was able to share Christ with them, and they placed their faith in Jesus. I baptized them that weekend. They have been faithful members ever since.

"I kept this up four days a week for about half a day each day. Five years later, I'm still doing it. Soon I got other people to come with me. The church grew. We added staff. One of my requirements for staff is that they must be willing to spend half their time knocking on doors. *That's* how we doubled the church twice in the last five years."

Is this the only way to grow a church? Absolutely not! I think one of the smartest things I've heard Rick Warren say was, "It takes all kinds of churches to reach all kinds of people."

Visitation isn't for everybody. It's certainly not the only way to grow a group or a church. In fact, it's worth remembering that we're wrapping up a section called "Things That Matter *Some*."

We're about to get into things that matter a lot. Pound for pound, we have methods that more positively and consistently predict growth than visitation. But if you love to visit people and you're good at it, don't let anyone discourage you. Don't let anyone tell you that your way is old-fashioned and that it can't work anymore.

This principle applies to more than just visitation. There are lots of methods that have been discarded because some pundit decided they were old-fashioned and didn't work anymore, and so we quit doing them. But here's the real reason many methods don't work: We don't *work* them.

Visitation is not the only way to grow a group, nor is it even necessarily the best way, but it *is* a good way. If you're positively disposed to do visitation, do it with all your heart.

Now, let's move to those things that mattered a **lot**.

section two

what makes groups grow— a lot

introduction

We can't concentrate on everything. Success in life is about concentrating on the things that really matter and doing them well. And in terms of making your groups grow, four things made it onto the "this really matters" list.

What does it take to make the list? I set the criteria at 100 percent difference between the bottom groups and the top groups. Groups using these practices are twice as likely (or more) to be growing as those not using them.

These factors also tend to have a layering effect. Just as additional layers of plywood strengthen all the plywood together, the more layers you've got, the stronger your support. Groups characterized by two or three of the following qualities were far more likely to be growing than those marked by only one of these practices.

C. Peter Wagner tells about attending horse pulls when he was young. One of the strongest horses could pull 7,000 pounds, another an amazing 9,000 pounds. But when the two horses were hitched together, they could pull 33,000 pounds.[1]

The same principle is true when it comes to growing groups. There is a compounding, layering effect. If you want to grow a group, the following pages will tell you how to start doing it—or do it even better. We've got the stats and the success stories to back it up. So let's read on.

the group that parties together grows together

Y es, parties matter *that* much.

Groups that have nine or more parties a year are 104 percent more likely to be growing than low-fellowship groups—groups that have four or fewer gatherings a year. The group that parties together grows together.

So it's time to take parties seriously—at least in terms of helping your groups grow. Have fun, and be intentional about it.

Parties can, and should, take on a wide variety of forms:

- Short and long: Parties can be Sunday brunch or a weekend retreat.
- Expensive and cheap: Usually cheap is better, and it's easier to do often. But for a Valentine's Day dinner, a sit-down restaurant might work better than a fast-food joint.
- Guy events and gal events: Stereotypically, these parties might be sporting events for guys and shopping for the ladies. But do whatever works best for your particular group.
- Fun events, as well as service events: Ministry and outreach projects can be included in this list.

- Seasonal events, such as New Year's parties
- Anytime events: Have a party *just because.*

There are biblical reasons, as well as sociological ones, why groups that party together grow together. Let's look at the biblical reasons first.

Levi's strategy

Someone came up to me after a conference and said, "What you're talking about isn't really a church program. What you are talking about is just Christian living." I'd like to look at this issue of hospitality from that perspective. I believe if we live the Christian life the way the Bible says to live it, our groups will grow. And parties are biblical!

A party was Levi's strategy. "Later, Levi held a banquet in his home with Jesus as the guest of honor. Many of Levi's fellow tax collectors and other guests also ate with them" (Luke 5:29).

I'm not sure the word *banquet* completely conveys the idea. Look at the description in other translations:

- *great banquet* (NIV)
- *large reception* (GWD)
- *big dinner* (CEV)
- *big feast* (TEV)
- *great feast* (ASV)
- *big reception* (NASB)

Sounds like Levi knew how to throw a party!

You get the impression that many of these guests became followers of Jesus, even though the Pharisees didn't like Jesus' party plan too well.

Get into the habit

I believe one of the best ways to study the Bible (and to teach the Bible) is by bombarding the text with questions. So let's try this text on for size: "Get into the habit of inviting guests home for dinner" (Romans 12:13, TLB).

What's the nature of the language in this verse? Let's make this multiple choice.

___ prophecy
___ proverb
___ parable
___ command

You know the answer. It's a command. As surely as God commanded us to pray or give or serve, God has commanded us to get into the habit of inviting guests home for dinner.

In the Greek, this entire passage is actually only two words, which can be translated as "pursue hospitality." *Pursue* means to chase or hunt. It's an active word. It can be used in the sense of persecute. It's an aggressive word. There's nothing passive about the way we're to go about being hospitable. The Greek word, which we might translate as "hospitality," actually has a more complex meaning. It comes from two words—*phileo*, "to love," and *xenia*, "strangers."[1] Thus, to show hospitality is to love strangers. If it's just your friends, it's not *fully* biblical hospitality. So be sure to invite people you don't know, too.

Paul's words in Romans suggest a process, something that happens over time. As The Living Bible says, "Get into the habit." It's not a one-time event—it's a way of life. Christian living is, in part, about getting into the habit of inviting guests home for dinner. The New Living Translation puts it, "Always be eager to practice hospitality." Practice. Like a doctor practicing medicine. The doctor keeps practicing throughout his career.

Success in almost any arena of life is a result of habits. If we are constantly having to remind ourselves and force ourselves to do something, we're probably not doing it regularly. We need to get to the point where it's a reflex action. We need to make it the normal thing to do Friday night, Sunday midday, or whenever it is we'd like to regularly practice hospitality.

Someone once asked me, "What if I don't like inviting guests home for dinner? Could I take them to Applebee's instead?"

I thought it was a silly question, but he was dead serious. After talking to quite a number of Christians about this, I find it's an issue over which some in the body of Christ are truly divided. Some see it this way: The Bible says, "home." I believe it means *home*. And that settles it: It is "home."

Others see it differently. I spoke with a widowed man whose wife had passed away six months earlier. He told me that in those six months, he hadn't eaten a single home-cooked meal. Not one. I don't know about you, but I'm not sure I'd *want* to go to his house for dinner! I think Applebee's might fit within the spirit of the law in this case.

Still, the Bible does say "home," so let's use that as our default for this chapter. In one of my follow-up surveys, I asked, "When was the last time you had guests at your home for dinner or dessert?" Eighty-five percent of the respondents were in one of two categories—either they had dinner or dessert guests within the last three months or it had been a year or more since they had guests for dinner. Most people either do hospitality regularly or not at all. The Bible says to make it a habit.

So what can we expect to happen when we invite guests home for dinner? If you haven't done this much, you might first of all expect that they'll show up. I've invited guests over quite often, and I can tell you that sometimes they'll come and sometimes they won't. Sometimes they say they'll come, and then they won't. Sometimes they'll come, and you'll have a grand time. Sometimes they'll come, and they'll be boring. Sometimes they'll come and be obnoxious. And sometimes they'll come and won't leave.

Once we had a house full of people, and everyone had a good time and stayed until 10 or 11. Everyone except one guy. He stayed and stayed and stayed. I stopped putting wood on the fire about midnight. I pretty much stopped talking about 1:00 a.m. I think he left sometime after 2:00 a.m. This brings us to the next verse I'd like us to consider.

Hospitality without grumbling

"Offer hospitality to one another without grumbling" (1 Peter 4:9, NIV).

Let's look at this passage the way we did the verse from Romans—by asking, What's the nature of the language here?

Again, it's a command. And not an isolated command, either; it's repeated. Our sovereign, holy Lord, boss, and God commanded us to offer hospitality. And to not grumble about it.

Someone once asked me, "What if I don't like inviting guests home for dinner?" My response was, "Repent, sinner! God *said* to do it!" Not in that exact language, of course. But I do make the point that this is something we're *commanded* to do. Christian living is done together, in each other's lives and in each other's homes.

What if I were to describe a best friend to you, tell you all about him, and then say, "But funny thing—he's never been to my home"? It's impossible for me to imagine a best friend who had not been to my home dozens of times. There's something about sharing each other's space that draws us closer together.

Next question: Why? Why are we to offer hospitality without grumbling? I can think of two reasons.

1) We're to offer hospitality without grumbling because all good ideas can degenerate into work. When we have people over, my wife is pretty dialed up about having the house clean. And when I say she likes having the house clean, I mean she likes having the *whole* house clean. She likes having the living room clean, the kitchen clean, the bedroom clean, the bedroom bathroom clean, the bedroom bathroom *shower* clean....

I've tried explaining to her, "Sweetie, I don't think they're going to take a shower."

"I know, I know," she says. "It just makes my soul feel at peace when the house is clean."

I've never quite understood this. But I understand *this*: When Momma ain't happy, ain't nobody happy. So when we have people over, I always make a point to help clean up. I'll clean the shower or mow the lawn or buy the Diet Coke or make the coffeecake.

After service one week, I invited four new couples to join our group the next Friday evening. I called them on Monday and called back on Thursday to confirm. Friday afternoon I was doing what I always do—vacuuming the floor, taking out the trash, running to the store, cleaning up the shower (yes, I know). Seven o'clock rolled around. Our friends showed up, but not one of the four couples I had invited came. Around 7:30, I got on the phone and called one of them.

"Ron, this is Josh from the church. We talked last night…"

"Oh yeah, Josh, sorry we didn't make it. I had a hectic day at the office. I was all stressed out and just felt like chillin' at the house tonight. Sorry."

"Ron. You need to come look at my bathroom. I have been shining this thing up just for *you*." That was what I was tempted to say. But I needed to remember what the Bible says: "Offer hospitality to one another without grumbling." We need to remember that hospitality *is* hospitality, not just a task we have to complete.

2) We are to offer hospitality without grumbling because… well, some people are kind of hard to love. I had been talking all evening at a conference in Oklahoma about using hospitality to grow groups. Afterward, a man came up to me and reflected, "Some people here in Oklahoma are kind of hard to love." Indeed. In fact, it's not just true in Oklahoma; it's true of people everywhere.

Often when we say we want to win our world for God, what we mean is that we want to win nice people, funny people, interesting people. But that's not the world God sends us into. God has called us to reach all kinds of people, and sometimes they are hard to love.

God wants to make us into loving people. To do that, he puts into every church and every group someone who's an extra-grace-required kind of person—someone who's a little odd. Someone who's not that interesting, not that funny, not that fun to be with. Every group has one. Every church has a few, if not many. If you're thinking, That's not true of *our* group; everyone in our group is easy to love, I have some bad news—that person might be you!

My favorite speaker is John Ortberg, and my favorite of the stories he shares on the road relates to the difficulties of loving everyone. John tells about a time he was traveling by plane with his family from coast to coast.

It's a five-hour trip, and they felt crowded in their assigned seats. I'm picturing some lap children squirming and jabbering.

John noticed that there was quite a bit of room at the very back of the plane. So, he and his wife gathered their belongings and went to the back of the plane where they could spread out. An hour later, there was stuff strewn everywhere. The kids were crawling over the seats and under the seats. There were toys and blankets and rattles and snacks and pacifiers and stuff everywhere. (You know you're in trouble when the flight attendant comes by and says, "Can these kids play outside?")

After a while a guy came by. He surveyed the damage and said to John, "Hey. Are these your kids?" Startled, John replied, "Yeah."

The man got real serious and said, "I would do anything if I just had two kids."

John didn't know what to say. "I guess you and your wife are not able to have kids?"

"No, no. We have five kids. I would do anything if we just had *two* kids. Any two. Two would be plenty. I know this looks like a mess to you, but to me, it is a walk in the park."

Sometimes we feel that way about our kids. Sometimes we feel that way about the people in our group. Sometimes we'll have someone over for a party, and we'll feel that way about that person. Some people are hard to love. But it's our job to love them anyway.

Jesus taught us, "Your love for one another will prove to the world that you are my disciples" (John 13:35). Note that he didn't say people will know you are his disciples because you are so disciplined or you go to church all the time or are so spiritual. Our ability to love one another—including hard-to-love people—is the proof that we're walking with Jesus.

Who are we to invite?

Once we get into the habit of inviting guests home for dinner, who should we invite? When we offer hospitality to one another without grumbling, who are we to offer it *to*?

Jesus answered this question for us, too. "Then he told the man who had invited him, 'When you invite people for lunch or dinner, don't invite only your friends' " (Luke 14:12a, GWD).

Jesus' answer is rendered even more forcefully in other translations:

- "Then he turned to his host. 'When you put on a luncheon or a banquet,' he said, 'don't invite your friends' " (NLT).
- "Then Jesus said to his host, 'When you give a luncheon or dinner, do not invite your friends' " (NIV).

Did Jesus mean don't invite your friends at all? I have a son who'd say, "That doesn't sound very 'Jesus-ical' to me." Indeed, it doesn't sound like something Jesus would say. What's going on here?

I think the framers of God's Word translation captured the spirit of what Jesus was communicating. It's a hyperbole—an exaggeration to make a point. Jesus isn't saying it's sinful to ever invite your friends over for dinner. He's saying that on a regular basis—as a habit—we're to include outsiders. The normal thing for a Christian is to invite people we don't really know.

Have you ever invited friends over for dinner, or gone to dinner with some friends, without inviting any outsiders? All of us have. And I think that's OK sometimes. It's just that we shouldn't live that way all the time. On a regular basis, we should include people who aren't in our normal circle of friends at our dinners.

Why? Why is this so important? I want us to look at two sociological reasons why hospitality is so powerful.

Social proof

Robert B. Cialdini wrote an excellent book titled *Influence: The Psychology of Persuasion.* One of his six key sources of influence is what he calls social proof. We are profoundly influenced by the choices and decisions of the people in our group. Whatever our group wears, drives, and eats, we tend to wear, drive, and eat.[2] People like to buy bestselling books, drive popular cars, and eat at crowded restaurants.

I've seen this phenomenon for myself, in a few different ways. I received an offer once from Brian Tracy, who sells self-help books, CDs, videos, and various downloadable products. His offer was that if I would purchase his new book on amazon.com on a certain day, he would give me $250 of downloadable product for free. Now, why would Brian Tracy give me $250 worth of product for buying a $20 book? I'm sure his goal was to be the number 1 book on Amazon for that one day. He knew that if he could get to number 1 on that day, many would be influenced to buy the book.

I did an experiment of my own to test the power of social proof. I ride a shuttle nearly every week from long-term parking at El Paso International Airport to the terminal. When I first started doing this, I wasn't sure if the shuttle was a complimentary service provided by the airport or a situation where you were expected to tip the driver. I noticed most people didn't tip, so I didn't tip. Then I noticed a guy tipping, so I thought I should, too. Ever since then, I've been on a personal mission to raise the standard of living of the shuttle drivers at the El Paso airport.

Recently I decided to test my influence. I waited until we were about halfway back to the long-term parking lot before I got out any money. At this point, no one on the shuttle had any tip money out. I opened my wallet and pulled out a few dollars. I put the money conspicuously on my knee. I watched the couple across the shuttle from me. In a minute or two, the woman noticed the dollar bills in my hand. She looked like a fish circling the bait. She nudged her husband and whispered and pointed. He got a couple of bucks out of his wallet and held them in his hand. The person next to me was facing forward and not looking at me. But when the person across from us pulled out some money, he followed suit. Then another and another. Everyone on that shuttle gave the driver a tip.

Can I be sure that my influence caused that? Perhaps not, but countless research projects have demonstrated that we're profoundly influenced by the behavior of the people around us. As parents, we know this. We tell our teenagers, "Don't run with that crowd." We know that if they *do* run with that crowd, they'll start to walk and talk and dress and behave like that crowd.

The Bible speaks of this. "Blessed is the man who does not walk in the counsel of the wicked or stand in the way of sinners or sit in the seat of mockers" (Psalm 1:1). The man is blessed because he doesn't walk in the counsel of the wicked or stand in the way of sinners or sit in the seat of mockers and therefore doesn't start to think and act like the wicked, the sinners, and the mockers. Likewise, 1 Corinthians 15:33b says, "Bad company corrupts good character"(NIV).

The same principle can work positively. Surround your average pre-Christian with six or eight truly committed Christians—people who love the Lord with all their hearts, souls, minds, and strength—and everything changes.

I show a clip from an old *Candid Camera* episode in my conferences. It's called "Face the Rear." A number of members of the *Candid Camera* staff are on an elevator, all facing the rear of the elevator. One person after another steps into the elevator, looks around, sees everyone else facing the rear and, predictably, faces the rear, as well.

Andy Stanley, pastor of North Point Community Church in North Atlanta and son of Charles Stanley, talks about how they put this dynamic to work at North Point. When people from his church ask, "Is it OK to have non-Christians in our small group?" he replies, "Absolutely. And watch them change before your very eyes. And sure, they're going to come in with both feet on the brakes, and all kinds of preconceived ideas about theology and what you're up to, but just love them and involve them and watch the resistance fade."

We are profoundly influenced by the behavior of the people in our group. If unchurched, not-yet Christian people come to our groups, everything changes for them. And as we engage in the process of helping others grow, we grow, too.

An epidemic of loneliness

There is a second sociological reason why groups that have frequent parties are more likely to grow.

Quite a bit of research has been done in recent years about an epidemic of loneliness that has swept our nation. Perhaps the definitive work on the subject is *Bowling Alone* by Robert Putnam. Here is a summary of his findings:

During the first two-thirds of the [twentieth] century Americans took a more and more active role in the social and political life of their communities—in churches and union halls, in bowling alleys and clubrooms, around committee tables and card tables and dinner tables. Year by year we gave more generously to charity, we pitched in more often on community projects, and (insofar as we can still find reliable evidence) we behaved in an increasingly trustworthy way toward one another. Then, mysteriously and more or less simultaneously, we began to do all these things less often.[3]

Putnam provides hard data in the form of 40 or so charts in the back of the book. In category after category, from bowling leagues to PTA and playing cards with our friends, you can see the trend. Up, up, up for 65 years and then downward over the past 40 years. The result is an epidemic of loneliness.

The impacts of that epidemic are devastating. A study of a random sample of almost 7,000 residents of Alameda County, California, showed that people who lacked social and community ties were more than twice as likely to die during the nine years of the study. The relationship between social ties and longer life was found to be independent of other risk factors, such as smoking, obesity, and lack of exercise.[4] As John Ortberg puts it, "It is better to eat Twinkies with good friends than to eat broccoli alone."[5]

Doctors in another study, published in the *Journal of the American Medical Association*, subjected more than 270 people to a virus that causes the common cold. The "volunteers with the most ties to relatives, friends and community were the least likely to catch a cold."[6] Again, to quote Ortberg, "Unfriendly people are snottier than friendly people."

Putnam describes the change he documented as a loss of social capital. The result is an epidemic of loneliness and the depression that accompanies it. Martin Seligman, author of *Authentic Happiness*, wrote that depression was 10 times as prevalent as it was in 1960 and struck at a much younger age. The mean age of a person's first episode of depression almost 50 years ago was 29.5; in 2001 it was 14.5.[7]

The result of all of this is an opportunity—and a *need*—for the gospel to be heard in ways it's never been heard before.

A lesson from the mission field

I grew up a missionary kid in the Philippines. Missions 101 states that you use the felt needs of the culture to reach the culture. Therefore, if we find a culture hungry for physical bread, the people are far more likely to listen to the parable of the Bread of Life if we give them some regular bread first. If you try to go at it the other way, it doesn't work so well. "I know you're so hungry you think you're going to die, but we're *all* going to die, and when we do, we'll all stand before God. Are you ready to stand before God?"

Here in America, the great need of the hour is not for physical bread. If you were a missionary coming to America, you could read books like *Bowling Alone*. Or you could just listen to the radio. For a generation, we've listened to the Burt Bacharach, Hal David song, "What the world needs now is love, sweet love."

The lyrics raise an interesting question. If the world needs love and people know they need love, why don't they *get some*? Listen to the radio again—they're looking for love in all the wrong places.

And we in the church have that love. Most churches are reasonably loving places. If we'll love the world in the same way we love each other, we can win our world for Jesus.

Love is often very ordinary. It is a cup of coffee and table games and card-playing and laughter. It's the way you treat your friends and the way you make *new* friends.

So have a party once a month. And, as Jesus said, don't invite only your friends. If we make this one simple adjustment, we'll be twice as likely to be growing.

And if we throw parties as a team, we'll be three and a half times more likely to be growing. But that's the subject for another chapter. The next one.

chapter 4

go team!

What did Jesus say would be the bottleneck of the evangelistic/disciple-making process? What's keeping the gospel from spreading as rapidly as it could, according to Jesus? What is it we need so that we can make disciples of all nations? What is the most urgent need of the hour?

Workers.

Jesus taught that the bottleneck in the whole process was laborers (see Luke 10:2). We need workers. He didn't say we need leaders (although one could argue that leaders find workers); he said we need *workers*. And this illustration from Jesus' time meant day laborers, farm workers, people who sweat when they work. Leadership is only beneficial if it helps locate and create workers; otherwise, *all* your workers are leaders. And if you've been in meetings where everyone's trying to lead—and usually in several different and often conflicting directions—you know the end result often isn't pretty. Vision statements, mission statements, strategy-planning sessions, and all the rest are very nice, but the bottom line is, How many workers did we employ and *deploy*?

Big team=big growth

Groups that have a big team are more than twice as likely (115 percent) to be growing, compared with those with a small team. For my survey, I defined a big team as one with four or more people. A small team was the teacher and one other person. The more people you have helping you, the more likely it is that you'll grow. The results are quite linear. The following chart shows the percentage of groups that are growing in proportion to the number of people actively helping the group grow. The more people we have helping, the more likely the growth:

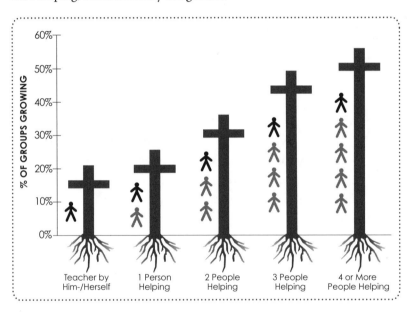

When we combine this factor with the one in our last chapter, the results are even more stunning. Groups with lots of parties (nine or more a year) *and* a large team are nearly five times as likely to be growing, compared with those who have four or fewer parties a year and a small team.

This is significant because it is so objective. These are things you can just *do*. The next chapter will get into the importance of people skills, which as important as they are, are harder to quantify and execute. You may know good people skills when you see them, but they're not something you can easily put on an organizational chart or to-do list.

These first two qualities that matter a lot, however, *are* things you can put on the calendar. You *can* recruit people. You *can* pray and ask God to raise up workers and send them into the field (even if that field's your living room). And you *can* throw a party! Why *wouldn't* you?

If you're a group leader and want your group to grow, the first part of our answer is simple: Gather a big team, and have lots of parties. It's easy to conceptualize, and it's pretty easy to do.

In *Double Your Class,* this was my prescription: Invite every member and every prospect to every fellowship every month. But whether or not you invite every member and every prospect, the sheer presence of the parties and a large team makes growth extremely probable.

The implications for those who lead group ministries are huge. If you can lead your groups to have lots of parties (shoot for one a month), and have lots of people sharing the load with the parties and with the group, it's almost guaranteed that you'll have groups that are growing.

So let's get back to focusing on teams. Who are we to recruit? And how are we to recruit them?

Pray as you go

Jesus didn't leave us in the dark as to how to do this. The second half of Luke 10:2 tells us, "So pray to the Lord who is in charge of the harvest; ask him to send more workers into his fields." We need to ask God to provide the people he needs to do the work. We can't convince people to serve unless God moves in their hearts.

In the next verse, Jesus said an interesting thing. "Now go, and remember that I am sending you out as lambs among wolves" (verse 3). Jesus told the disciples to pray, and then he told them to *go.* We, too, should follow Jesus' instruction. We should pray and go. We should make teams that will pray and go. We should ask God's help and then get on with what God's already asked us to do. One complements and fulfills the other.

We think of prayer as talking to God, but sometimes God speaks to us in prayer. My wife told me recently that she felt God speaking to her as she prayed. Her prayer was along these lines: "Lord, encourage Evelyn during this difficult time." She felt God was saying to her, "OK. I will encourage her. And I will use *you*. Buy her some flowers." The next day, we bought flowers for Evelyn.

Christianity is both active and passive. It is "let go and let God," and it is striving, running, pushing, straining. It is resting and receiving, and it is going and doing. We pray like it all depends on God, and we work like it all depends on us.

Jesus taught us to pray and go. From another perspective, he told us to pray and tell others to go—pray and recruit. Then he told us a little about what to expect. "Now go, and remember that I am sending you out as lambs among wolves" (Luke 10:3).

Have you ever heard someone recruit by saying, "Please help us; it won't be that much trouble"? That's not the way Jesus recruited, and it's not the way we should recruit. Jesus told his disciples it would be tough. Jesus told them it would be hard. Jesus told them there would be disappointments. We should, too.

Besides, we lie when we say, "It won't be that much trouble." It *will* be trouble. It will be work. It will take time and lots of it. There will be disappointment. Do you know what we get when we tell people it won't be that much trouble?

Not much. And that often leads to more trouble than we would have had if we'd simply been upfront about what we were asking of people.

When we recruit people, we need to be honest about the difficulties they might face. We need to explain that people will hurt their feelings and disappoint them, that it will probably take longer and be more trouble than they imagine. But we also need to remind them of something even more important than their feelings.

Bear in mind, though, that Jesus didn't say all this during his first conversation with his disciples. The first conversation was simply, "Follow me" (Matthew 4:19; Luke 5:27). Only much later did Jesus say, "Take up your cross and follow me" (Matthew 16:24; Luke 9:23). And it was even later that he said, "Now go, and remember that I am sending you out as lambs among wolves" (Luke 10:3).

There was a progression to Jesus' teaching. It started with an invitation to follow, and proceeded toward, "Now go, and remember that I am sending you out as lambs among wolves." There are two mistakes we must avoid. One is to call for too much commitment too early. The other is to ask for too little too late.

Turns out Jesus was right. Getting workers is a huge factor in growing a group. So now let's look at the data and find out exactly *how* huge.

Who are the players on my team?

John Maxwell said, "One is too small a number to achieve greatness."[1] We need a team to help us. But what does a team look like?

In my experience, a team's look varies quite a bit from church to church. If you're a group leader, I'd encourage you to follow the leadership of your pastors in this. There are many good ways to organize groups. What follows are some general ideas that may be adapted to a wide variety of settings.

First, here are the roles I see growing groups using:

Teacher. This person presents the lesson most of the time. This person isn't necessarily the leader or facilitator of the group, although he or she could and often will be. One thing I've learned from working with thousands of teachers is, well, they like to teach. They're not much into coordinating and reminding and organizing and calling and planning parties. They tend to be the kind of people who like to just prepare and present. Give them a venue to do it in.

Teacher-in-training. Eventually growth will kill a small group. But not in a bad way. The fact is, if a group grows, eventually it's not small anymore. That's a mathematical reality. But it's not a bad thing. The teacher-in-training is the one being prepared to lead—or at least teach—a new group. This is the kind of person to whom Paul addressed 2 Timothy 2:2: "And the things you have heard me say in the presence of many witnesses entrust to reliable men who will also be qualified to teach others" (NIV).

The teacher-in-training should get regular opportunities to teach. He or she needs practice. The only way to learn how to teach is to teach. And as that person teaches, there's a very good chance that he or she will begin to develop a following. Some may actually come to like the teacher-in-training's style better. (If you're the teacher, don't take this personally; celebrate your success in training your teacher.) Everyone's growing confidence in your teacher-in-training will make things significantly easier when it comes time to start a new group.

And as it turns out, this factor alone is a pretty good predictor of growth. In a follow-up survey, I asked whether or not groups had a teacher-in-training. Groups that did were almost two and a half times more likely (146 percent) to be growing, compared with those that didn't have a teacher-in-training.

Notice that I'm not just talking about a substitute teacher here. We're talking about a teacher-*in-training*. Every time that person teaches, the group should know that he or she's the teacher-in-training. This is a subtle way of casting a vision that the group intends to grow—and that as it does, there will be the need to start a new group. And what's more, it's likely that this person will be leading that group.

Inreach coordinator. This person cares for the people in the group and invites every member to every gathering. He or she tends to be naturally caring and nurturing, with gifts of encouragement and mercy. This person has a gift for calling or e-mailing people and asking them why they missed group—and letting them know that they *were* missed. And at the other end of the phone or e-mail, people don't feel nagged—they feel loved.

Research shows that if we contact people in their first month of drifting out of life in the group, they're far more likely to come back into the group. In a larger group, you'll need several people for this role.

Outreach coordinator. This person is the outgoing, extroverted salesperson type, someone who has never met a stranger. Outreach coordinators have a heart for people who are far from God. They remind the group often of the importance of evangelism and outreach. They encourage people to invite their friends to parties. They call every potential member to invite each one to every party, every month. Again, in a larger group, you might need several of these people.

Service/missions coordinator. Many groups do an outside ministry project from time to time. This event might substitute for the monthly party. For some, helping other people is *more* fun than going to a party.

Events might include things like painting a children's room at church, passing out cold bottles of water at an event (didn't Jesus say something about giving out cups of water?), or offering a free car wash. For more ideas on servant evangelism projects, see servantevangelism.com.

Party coordinator. If you're not in the habit of having monthly parties, you might think it isn't necessary to have someone in charge. You might think you'll just get together and have some fun. And you might be right. Some fellowships—like lunch together after church—are simple enough that they don't need a lot of preparation and planning. Other gatherings—like a scavenger hunt or other themed party—require considerably more effort.

Parties are work. If you haven't coordinated one lately, you have no idea how much trouble it is to have fun. Someone has to set up the meeting area, put up the decorations, prepare the food, get the games ready, and do all the rest to make your party a success. The ladies often wind up with this role, but it's a good idea to get the men involved as well. Then men will naturally plan events that other men are more likely to attend.

Group Publishing's Ministry in the 21st Century series has hundreds of party ideas for small groups of all shapes and sizes—for adults, men, women, married couples, young adults—as well as literally thousands more practical ideas for group leaders, ranging from starting groups to getting them prepared for outreach. Take advantage of them.

Prayer coordinator. Groups are not just about learning; they're also about caring and sharing. And they're about keeping the focus on God. One of the ways we do that is to share prayer requests. The prayer coordinator normally leads this time. Many prayer coordinators also take the next step and e-mail prayer requests to the entire group. That way all members, whether or not they're in attendance, can keep up with and share in what's going on in the group.

Prayer time is both prayer *and* share. There may be more efficient ways of sharing information about what our needs are. But it's not about efficiency; it's about sharing and caring. It's about doing life together.

Care-group leader. Only large groups will need a care-group leader. Think of a care group as "the small group inside the large group." Many on-campus, Sunday-school-style groups can become quite large. When they do, dividing the larger group into care groups works well. Each care group will need a care-group leader. An inreach leader and an outreach leader for each group is also a good idea. It's my strong preference that care groups physically gather together at some point during the larger group time. That way, everyone can see one another, notice who's not there, and make sure someone gets in touch with that person and doesn't let him or her fall through the cracks.

Marv, who leads a group at First Baptist Church of Maryville, Illinois, follows the care-group model. The first Sunday it met, his group had eight people. Four years later, the group has 89 people, and the group is subdivided into about a dozen groups of fewer than 10. Marv's wife takes care of most of the ministry and organizational issues, while Marv takes care of the teaching. Each care group has a leader. Marv meets with the care-group leaders on Wednesday nights to go over the lesson for Sunday.

Likewise, parties are done both as an entire group and as individual care groups. They have parties once a month—some months the whole group comes together, while other months each care group gets together. The focus on relationship extends into the group time, as well. Marv uses about half of the group time to teach, and the teaching is followed by a time of "compare, share, prayer" in the care groups.

Children's workers. The most reachable people on the planet are kids. The vast majority of people who come to Jesus do so before they leave their teenage years. Kids represent the greatest opportunity for the spread of the gospel. Yet the most acute need for workers in nearly every church I'm in is in the children's area. We do well to continually encourage people to consider ministry to kids.

For many churches, children's ministry is the front door to the church. By planning a children's ministry that is the best hour in a kid's week, we can reach kids and, in doing so, reach their families. With kids, the fields are especially white unto harvest (see John 4:35). All we need are workers.

Kids can be a big issue, depending on the demographic of your group. If your group contains young married couples or single moms, I don't need to explain what a big deal it is. Whether they'll come to group or not is directly tied to how well their children are cared for. Even as we and our kids grow older, this issue has the potential to affect group attendance. For example, a couple recently dropped out of a group in our church just because their daughter needed them to watch their grandchild.

One other thought about kids. The goal is not merely that they're watched and kept out of trouble. The goal is that they're taught to love Jesus and his church. We lay the foundation for Christian maturity while people are still children. So find ways not only to occupy kids' time but also to get them occupied with Jesus.

My wife teaches children's workers and is a big fan of *Children's Ministry Magazine* (childrensministry.com). You'll find great ideas there for recruiting children's workers, as well as for teaching kids.

Class leader. This is the person who makes it all happen. This person coordinates the work of everyone else. He or she calls the outreach leaders, inreach leaders, and fellowship leaders to make sure everything's going as planned. This person is well-organized and has good people skills. He or she tends to be a detail person.

Some teachers will want to push back. They'll say, "I don't need a class leader—*I'm* the leader!" And that's fine, if they really want to lead. Often, they really don't. They just love to teach.

Occasionally, you'll have a match made in heaven—a husband who loves to teach and a wife who loves to take care of everything else (or the other way around). Life is easy when this happens. When it doesn't, we have to work a little harder to get a team together.

Vision Day

Again, the bottleneck of the evangelistic/disciple-making process is laborers. Jesus taught us that would be true. Yet people are nearly always surprised by this.

I speak in churches of all sizes. I've been in churches with multiple thousands in their small-group ministry and in churches with fewer than 100 members. The size doesn't matter; the problem is the same everywhere: "We just can't get enough workers!"

Small-church leaders will put it this way. "Josh, we're just so small.

There aren't very many of us. The same people have to do everything because we don't have enough workers."

Big-church leaders put it a different way. "Do you have any idea how much work it is to get inreach leaders, outreach leaders, fellowship leaders, teachers-in-training and all the rest in a church with 3,000 in groups? We have close to 300 groups! That's a lot of workers! We can't get enough workers."

Here's what I suggest: As a group, have a Vision Day once a quarter. Every three months, re-cast your group's vision. Talk about the progress your group has made and your goals and plans for the next quarter. (If you use materials that run on a quarterly basis, do this at the beginning of each quarter.) If there's a "numbers guy" in your group who can statistically illustrate your progress, all the better. Talk about what parties went well and why. Brainstorm ideas for future parties. Talk about who might be drifting and who needs some love and attention in the group, whether that's a one-on-one lunch or a group visit.

Then talk about who'd like to serve during the next quarter. Ask, "Who'd like to plan the fellowships?" "Who'd like to invite every member?" "Who'd like to invite every prospect?"

This quarterly evaluation is key to making your group grow. It provides ongoing midcourse corrections to keep your group on track.

It's been said that an airplane is technically off course about 99 percent of the time. That is, 99 percent of the time it's not heading straight toward its destination. Winds constantly blow it off course. Through a series of midcourse corrections—not too unlike what we do when we drive—the plane is able to arrive at its destination. Vision Days insure that you'll have regular midcourse corrections so you'll stay on track.

So what is the vision?

I'd suggest you have the same vision for your small group that Jesus had for his. He would often retreat from the crowds to relax with his small group of disciples. Jesus' primary ministry was that of small-group leader.

What vision did Jesus give to his small group? "Therefore, go and make disciples of all the nations, baptizing them in the name of the Father and the Son and the Holy Spirit. Teach these new disciples to obey all the commands I have given you. And be sure of this: I am with you always, even to the end of the age" (Matthew 28:19-20).

Jesus told his small group to make disciples of the entire planet, starting with their small group. We ought to adopt the same vision for our small groups. In fact, it should be the vision of every small group—to reach the entire planet, starting with the small group itself.

That may sound impossible to you. And that's OK. God's specialty is the impossible. I don't know if you've ever thought about it this way, but Christian living is largely about *embracing* the impossible.

So how can we reach the whole planet, starting with our small group? A group of 10 that doubles every 18 months would reach the entire planet in less than 44 years. How can we do that?

Start by doing what *is* possible. And then watch God take your faithfulness and work the *im*possible.

Groups that have lots of parties are twice as likely to be doubling as those that don't. Groups that have a large team helping with the parties are twice as likely to be growing. That's encouraging enough right there. And totally doable.

But remember: Groups that have lots of parties *and* have a large team are *nearly five times* as likely to be growing. What could that look like for your groups?

We want to embrace the vision of growing and multiplying. We want to have three fellowships in the next three months. We need inreach leaders, outreach leaders, party coordinators, and so forth. Who can affirm the gifting of those who can do these tasks? Who wants to try something new?

We learn by doing. We discover gifting by experimenting. Try something—you might like it!

Too much ministry is ministry by pronouncement. Leaders get in a room, close the door, and hash out all the options. Then they come out with an announcement (usually in the form of a PowerPoint presentation): "Here's what we've decided is best. Therefore, this is the way it's going to be." Leaders believe they know what's best for the foreseeable future, and we respect our leaders enough to believe them. Thus, the new plan has an air of permanence about it.

But the truth is, it's hard to make an accurate decision for those in the trenches if you haven't been there yourself. And many leaders, through no fault of their own, just haven't been there.

It's far better to dabble and experiment first. Try something for three months. Give it a chance to work, but don't commit to it long term just yet. See how it works. Then adjust the plan as needed.

"Plant your seed in the morning and keep busy all afternoon, for you don't know if profit will come from one activity or another—or maybe both" (Ecclesiastes 11:6). You don't always know what's going to work. So try lots of stuff and keep what works for your group.

People don't want to make long-term commitments to things they've never tried. The Vision Day approach means they won't have to. They only have to do a three-month trial. Let them help plan three parties in the next three months, and then talk about how it went and how they felt. Ultimately, you're trying to help them discover how God has gifted them.

Which role is right?

As your group members get closer to the sweet spot of their gifting, life will just get more and more rewarding. Not that it won't also get more interesting. They'll experience several recurring feelings as they get closer to the center of their calling. Anticipate these feelings, so you'll know how to handle them as they experience them.

They'll love what they do. This is probably the most fun one of the bunch. I used to think service was the hidden fine print of the Christian life. If I could have changed Christianity, I would have taken the service part out.

I have come to understand that serving Jesus is the good stuff—the best stuff, in fact. I wouldn't trade my serving Christianity for nonserving Christianity for anything. Life at its best is serving God the way he's built us to do it.

They'll find they're actually pretty good at it. You don't have to be Billy Graham to have a gift for evangelism. You don't have to be Mother Teresa to have a gift for service. But you do have to have some competence. If you have a gift for teaching and you teach, people learn. If you have a gift for mercy and you show compassion, people feel comforted. If you go to the hospital and people feel worse when you leave than they did when you came…well then, you probably don't have the gift of mercy. There will be some degree of competence in a person's area of gifting.

They'll think their gift is the most important one out there. Obviously, take care with pride issues on this one. Still, this feeling is a pretty good sign where a person's gifting and heart are.

People with the gift of teaching like to quote verses like, "The truth will set you free" (John 8:32) and, "be transformed by the renewing of your mind" (Romans 12:2, NIV). People with the gift of mercy like to quote sayings like, "People don't care what you know until they know that you care." Administrators like to talk about God's business. Part of what it means to be gifted is that you feel, deep in your gut, "*This* is what really matters." Whenever people say "This is what it's all about," you've been handed a clue to their true gifting.

They want leadership to care more about it. Again, watch out for pride issues and/or the impulse to disrespect or try to end-around authority on this. But if people care about something that much, it's usually a pretty good indicator of their gifting.

Administrators want their pastors to be CEOs of well-run businesses. Mercy people want their elders to do hospital visitation. Evangelists want the entire church to hit the streets. Teachers want people to show up for their studies. If you continually want to see more participation from others in a certain area, it's probably the area you're gifted in.

Serving God near the sweet spot of your gifting brings more delight and fulfillment than just about anything imaginable. And that fact raises a question: Why is recruiting even necessary? If it's so much fun and brings them so much joy, why don't people just naturally do it?

In many cases, it's because we fail to do one last thing.

Encourage your workers

Ministry can be hard. Jesus said it would be so. It's hard to be a lamb when you're among wolves.

Churches would do well to encourage the workers they have. If we'd work harder at encouraging the workers we have, we might not have to work so hard at replacing the ones that burn out. For that matter, fewer *existing* workers would burn out.

I saw a great example of this at an annual leadership appreciation dinner in Louisville, Kentucky. Dr. Hal Pettegrew, who at the time was minister of education at Walnut Street Baptist Church, invited me to speak there. They had really done it right. They had awards for just about everyone. Everyone whose group grew at all got a certificate. If you had 10.1 people last year and 10.2 this year, you received an award.

Walnut Street Baptist had awards for the fastest-growing groups, groups that sent out the most workers, and groups that saw the most people come to Jesus. (Children's groups tended to do best at this.) Hal didn't recognize just the leaders; whole teams received recognition. Leaders were given a bag a candy and told to celebrate with the entire group. The idea was to recognize that everyone was a winner.

One award really got my attention. It was the teachers' award—chosen by the teachers themselves. The winner was an elderly lady who'd been teaching forever. I was sitting nearby and watched her as she sat down after receiving the award. She rubbed her hand slowly back and forth across the piece of paper that read, "Teacher of the Year." I could hear her repeat quietly, "I can't believe they did this for me. I just can't believe it. No one has ever done anything like this before." She kept saying this over and over softly to herself, rubbing her hand back and forth across the piece of paper.

I have a guess. It's only a guess; I can't prove it. But I'm willing to bet that when this woman passes on and her kids rummage through her belongings, they'll find that piece of paper. She'll keep it the rest of her life. Such is the value of acknowledgement, and it's one of the primary ways we can reward others.

The Bible says, "Honor the officers of your church who work hard among you" (1 Thessalonians 5:12, TLB). Strictly speaking, this passage addresses how we treat our pastors, but the same principle applies more broadly. Reward is mostly about recognition and honor. We would do well to honor everyone who works hard among us.

We don't get what we ask for, long for, or hope for. We get what we reward. Your church is perfectly tuned to get the results you are getting through the things you are rewarding. If you want different results, reward different efforts.

If you want your group to grow, get a big team helping you. Recruit inreach leaders, outreach leaders, care-group leaders, children's workers, and all the rest. Have a Vision Day to allow people to dabble in various areas of ministry. Use this process to help people discover their spiritual gifts. Reward the people who help.

Strong people skills will help you in the task of recruiting people. That's the topic of our next chapter.

○ MAKE YOUR GROUP GROW

like your group—and show it

my "day job" is writing lessons for small groups. In fact, I'd argue that I've written more small-group lessons than anyone else, living or dead. I write four lessons a week and have done so for years.

My favorite kind of question is what I call a "jump-ball" question—a question that can legitimately be answered in either of two opposite ways. And if you ask it just right, you'll get half the group on one side and the other half of the group on the other side.

Here's one of my all-time-favorite questions: Should a Christian try to be popular?

Immediately, someone will say no. He or she will quote Galatians 1:10, "Obviously, I'm not trying to win the approval of people, but of God. If pleasing people were my goal, I would not be Christ's servant," or something similar. Someone else may point out the futility and counterproductiveness of trying to be popular by saying, "I don't even *like* people who try too hard to be popular."

On the other hand, I've known people—and you probably have, too—who were very dedicated, committed, and knowledgeable about the Bible and who lived a holy life in many ways and yet were almost useless to the work of God.

Why? Because no one liked them. They were grumpy and moody. When you saw these dedicated saints, you just wanted to walk the other way.

And let's not forget some other words from Paul: "I try to please everybody in every way. For I am not seeking my own good but the good of many, so that they may be saved" (1 Corinthians 10:33, NIV).

So there's tension in this question. How might we answer it in a way that satisfies both sides?

Jesus is our example. He never compromised. He stood for the truth, no matter how others responded. But was Jesus popular? Absolutely. He had a charisma and a love for people that drew them like a magnet. We would all do well to be like Jesus.

We should not only *love* our groups, but *like* them, as well. And we should behave in a way that *shows* our group members that we like them. Living a holy, openly joyful life in Jesus should attract people to Jesus, not drive them away. And treating others in a way that shows they matter to God and to us helps groups grow. The statistics prove it.

People skills matter

Groups led by those with strong people skills are two and a half times more likely (147 percent) to be growing, compared with groups led by those with poor people skills.

effects of people skills on growth

% OF GROUPS GROWING

People Skills Ranking: 1 · People Skills Ranking: 2 · People Skills Ranking: 3 · People Skills Ranking: 4 · People Skills Ranking: 5

The progression is completely linear. The better the people skills, the more likely the growth.

When combined with the previous two factors that matter a lot—parties and high involvement—the results are staggering. Sixty-nine percent of groups that have lots of parties, a high involvement, and high people skills are growing.

Of the groups that had few parties, low involvement, and poor people skills, *zero* reported growing. I couldn't find *one*.

It's not difficult to have parties, big teams, or even better people skills, but it does require being intentional. So get started, and make it happen! Your groups will thank you for it.

And here's even more good news: Strong people skills will not only increase the odds that your group will grow but also enhance just about every other area of your life.

Why develop people skills?

Tim Sanders has done extensive research on what he calls the Likeability Factor. Here are just a handful of the benefits of being likeable that he's found:

- Doctors spend more time with, and give better care to, patients they like.
- Success in the work place is not so much about what you know or who you know but your popularity.
- Jurors award higher settlements to likeable defendants.
- Likeable political candidates are more likely to be elected.
- Likeability is one of the most reliable predictors of happiness in marriage.[1]

Good people skills arguably have a more direct effect on success in more areas of life than anything else. People with good people skills generally make more money, have deeper friendships, have stronger families, are more successful at work, and serve God more effectively than people who have poor people skills.

Here's the real problem: People universally think they're doing better with people skills than they are. The admonishment in Romans 12:3, "Don't think you are better than you really are," applies to people skills as much as to any other area. We have a bad habit of thinking we are better at getting along with others than we are.

John Ortberg tells of a survey of 829,000 high school students who were asked these questions:

How would you rate yourself compared to other students in your ability to get along with other students? Would you say you are above average or below average?

What percentage of these high school students actually thought they were above average in their ability to get along with other people? Take a guess.

By definition, 50 percent should be above and 50 percent should be below average. The actual answer: 100 percent! One hundred percent of high school students said: I'm above average in my ability to get along with other people. Not only that, but 25 percent of high school students estimated that they were in the top 1 percent in their ability to get along with other people. It's not just high school students who have a problem with this. Take an academic setting. Ninety-five percent of all faculty members rated themselves as "Above Average" in their performance as teachers and scholars. These are real smart people.

People in the hospital as the result of an accident that they caused by driving badly rate themselves as "Above Average" drivers. More than 90 percent of preachers who have to talk about texts like Romans 12 where it says: Do not think of yourself more highly than you ought, but consider yourself with sober judgment; consider themselves to be "Above Average" preachers.

A last example: When this concept of a "Self-serving Bias" is explained to people so that they understand it, the vast majority of people say that they are above average in their ability to handle the "Self-serving Bias."[2]

Are we as skilled as we think?

Try a little experiment. E-mail 50 friends and ask them, "On a scale of 1 to 10, how would you rate your ability to get along with others?" See how many put themselves in the bottom half.

I did this myself as I was working on this chapter. Pretty quickly, I received 405 responses. Here's how they broke down:

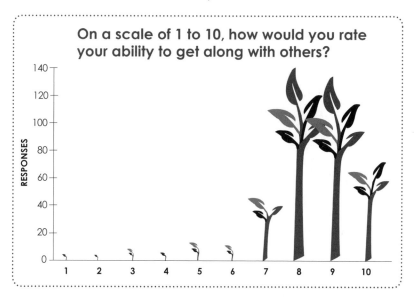

On a scale of 1 to 10, how would you rate your ability to get along with others?

Eighty-five percent of my friends rated themselves an 8 or higher. Think about that. By mathematical definition, if everyone's perception were 100 percent accurate, there would be the same number of 1s and 2s as there were 9s and 10s. And yet only 2 percent put themselves in the bottom half. Either my friends are very easy to get along with, or they're normal and they overestimate their ability to get along with others.

Check it out with your own friends. There's a good chance—a *very* good chance—that you think you're better at people skills than you are. There's a reason the Bible says not to think of yourself as better than you are. It's because we all have a tendency to do so.

What *are* good people skills?

I used to ski quite a bit when I was younger. Occasionally I'd get paired up with some arrogant soul who thought he was a great skier. He'd be all decked out in expensive gear, talking the lingo. So I'd ask him about his day.

"Looks like you have some pretty impressive gear there. Are you a pretty good skier?"

"Yeah, I guess you could say that."

"Have you been down Geronimo?

"No, too icy for me."

"What about Wild Onion?"

"Too steep for my taste."

"Have you checked out Capitan?"

"Too many moguls."

"What about Roy's Run?"

"No, I don't do the deep powder."

Right about this time, I began thinking, So let me get this straight. You're a good skier who can ski well on slopes that are not too steep, don't have too many moguls, and where the snow is not too deep or too icy. So as long as we're on a smooth, medium-grade, well-groomed slope, you can really tear it apart, right?

A good skier can ski well in all kinds of conditions. Likewise, having good people skills means having the ability to get along with almost any-one—young or old, educated or not, obnoxious or boring or self-absorbed or talkative or shy or arrogant or narcissistic or any other personality trait you don't like dealing with.

By the way, how many narcissists does it take to change a light bulb? One—he just holds the bulb while the whole world revolves around him. But amazingly, people with good people skills learn to get along with these people, too.

The Bible says we are to be "quick to listen, slow to speak and slow to get angry" (James 1:19, NIV). Following this advice will go a long way toward improving people skills. How exactly do we do this? Here are some ideas I've picked up along the way that will help.

The one-second pause

A habit that will immediately improve your conversational skills is remembering to take a one-second pause before you speak. That's it. Breathe. Wait. One second. Make sure the other person is finished before you speak.

Well-trained telephone customer-service representatives practice the one-second pause. They never interrupt. Never. They wait one second. Maybe two. They make sure you have finished saying what you wanted to say before they begin speaking. The conversation may even seem a bit awkward if you're used to the pace of someone who constantly steps on the ends of your sentences, but it's refreshing to feel like you're actually being heard by another human being.

The opposite is as irritating as it is common—feeling like you're not being heard because people start in on what they have to say before you're half-finished with your last sentence. How did they know it was your last sentence? Their interruption made sure it was.

So be sure to practice this one-second-pause habit in your group. Listen. Pause. Wait. Make sure the other person has said what he or she needed to say. Skilled leaders and teachers model this. When someone shares, they listen and never interrupt.

Sometimes, however, other people in the group *will* interrupt. What then? As a leader, what do I do when Bob interrupts Jim midsentence? Do I call Bob down in the middle of group time? A better approach is to wait until Bob is finished. Wait one more second, and then turn back to Jim and ask, "Were you finished with what you had to say, Jim?" Hopefully, Bob takes the hint. If he doesn't, *then* you might want to chat with him privately.

You might also talk to the group about the one-second pause before starting your group time. Talk about the vision of a group where everyone can be heard and how something as simple as a one-second pause can help accomplish it. Truth is, it will not only make a better group, but it will help your group members in *all* their relationships.

Repeat what you've heard

Here's another one you can learn from customer-service reps. They always restate the problem. My conversation with them may go something like this:

"My DSL isn't working."

"What seems to be the problem?"

"I can't connect to the Internet."

(Pause to make sure I am finished.)

"What I'm understanding, Mr. Hunt, is that the DSL at your home is not working and you can't connect to the Internet."

Exactly! It feels great to be heard! Companies spend piles of money teaching their employees these little tricks. You can use them, too. At no charge.

This is a great method to use in your group. When someone raises a concern, repeat it in your own words: "What I hear you saying is…." Your group members will feel they've been heard, and by putting what they said in your own words, you'll have learned something about them in a deeper way, too.

Empathize

Let's continue our conversation with the customer service representative:

"Yes, my DSL doesn't work."

"I'm sorry, you must feel really frustrated."

Yes! I am *so* frustrated! You get me! You really *get* me! I feel like hiring my DSL reps to be my counselors. It feels good to be understood. I feel good when my feelings are validated. My rep knows exactly how I feel and cares that I'm frustrated. By the time I've had the chance to process the fact that this is all just good training and not necessarily sincere empathy, we're already on our way to fixing the problem.

Occasionally, someone will really open up. When that happens, simply restating the problem isn't enough. Recently I was in a group where one gentleman began to share about his pain growing up. It's inappropriate to give the details here, but suffice it to say that during the course of sharing, he broke down and cried. The ladies cried. *I* cried. When he finished, there was this awkward silence. No one knew quite what to do.

Finally, I stood up and walked over to him. I placed my hands on his shoulders and simply asked the group, "Would you join me in prayer?" Boy, did we pray. It was a powerful moment for all of us.

Group life is about creating moments. Moments of reality. Moments of transparency. Moments when God is there. Moments when people are real and open up and support each other in true Christian empathy and love. It just doesn't get any better than that.

But you have to slow down. You have to listen. You have to pause. You have to empathize.

Ask questions—lots of questions

The easiest people to get along with are talkers. You just nod and grunt every now and then, and they think you're brilliant. Here's an old saying worthy of consideration: If a gossip is someone who talks about others all the time and a bore is someone who talks about himself or herself all the time, what do you call someone who talks about *you* all the time? A brilliant conversationalist!

The most difficult people for me to get along with are nontalkers. They speak with one-word sentences—and usually one-syllable words: Yes. No. No. Yes. No. These folks will tax your brain. But people with good people skills can cultivate a conversation with them, just as good skiers can ski all kinds of terrain and conditions.

When I'm in this situation, I remember the writer's six friends: Who? What? Where? When? Why? And How? Try to lead people into open-ended why and how questions that can't be answered with one word. Here are a few basic examples:

- What were you thinking or feeling when that happened?
- How were you able to get out of that situation?
- Why do you think he did that?

Once you've asked questions, follow up with more questions. And then ask more questions.

Use two "egg timers"

These aren't real egg timers, mind you. But my recommendation is to have two in your brain—one to time how much you talk and the other to time how much the other person talks. Keep an approximate running total of both. Make sure the other person is talking more than you are—but not *too* much more.

If you do most of the talking, the other person will think you're boring. I know, that's hard to imagine. But if you do most of the listening, he or she will think you're brilliant. Ask a few questions and nod for an hour, and people will walk away saying what an interesting person you are.

It's important, though, to have *some* degree of balance. It's shocking how many people will dominate 95 percent of the conversation if you let them. It's also rude, wrong, and usually nonproductive. Don't let it go there. Use your mental egg timers to ensure that *neither* side is dominating the conversation.

Here's one idea you can use your own judgment with. When I'm in a long conversation with someone and he or she is doing all the talking and I'm asking all the questions, I'll change tactics. It may sound a little rude, but if the egg timers are way out of balance, I'll say to myself, It's time for that person to listen to *me* for a while, and I'll dive in. If the other person doesn't have the good sense to take turns, I'm going to help him or her out. And I'll introduce my half of the conversation to…well… *the conversation.*

Again, feel free to disagree with me on this last point, but I believe it helps the conversation become healthier and more constructive.

Get below the surface

Discussions follow a certain progression of subject matter. First come the facts, then opinions, and then, finally, feelings.

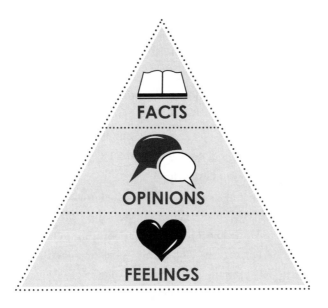

If you just stay on the facts, the conversation isn't going to be that interesting. Peel back the layers of the onion. Ask, "What did you think about that?" (Opinion). Then, if it's appropriate, go deeper: "How do you feel about what he did?" (Feeling).

Start with facts, go to opinions, and then to feelings. Don't skip levels. And don't get stuck at a level. Move from one level to another regularly. We can move through the levels slowly, but we need to move through them. People with good people skills know when it's appropriate to go deeper and when the conversation needs to simmer a bit. Surface conversations are not that satisfying for anyone. But don't try to go too deep too fast.

Find something in common

We naturally feel better about people with whom we have something in common. One meaning of the word *fellowship* is "mutual sharing" and speaks of the fact that we have a common relationship with Jesus. Because of that, we have a common relationship with each other. The more we find we have in common, the easier it is to get along.

Life is so complex that if you look hard enough, you can find common ground with almost anyone. Look for it. Find it. And then occupy it. Together.

I recently accepted the call to a very small church in the country. When

I say country, I mean *country*. From the church property, I couldn't hit a man-made structure in any direction, even with a golf ball and a club. That's a bit of an exaggeration, but it's not that far from true.

I'm pretty much a city boy. Not a big-city boy—a medium-sized-city boy. I like a town that's big enough to have a Best Buy and a Barnes & Noble, but not so big as to have gridlock.

The people in my congregation are country folk—farmers with dirt under their fingernails. I overheard one of them make fun of a city boy who said that he loved golf because he loved the great outdoors. The city boy's statement made sense to me. Not to them. Golf is a city sport, from their viewpoint. You have to go to the city to go to a golf course. You don't go to a golf course to see the great outdoors. You sit on your front porch and do that.

Country folks are different. They wave at everybody when they drive—mostly, I think, because they know everybody. When you ask where they live, they don't give an address you can plug into your GPS; they talk about where they live in reference to somewhere else. "Do you know where the rock wall is on the way to the church? Turn left there." Sometimes I wonder if they actually *know* their own street addresses.

Country folks tend to be real handy. The men know how to fix things. The women know how to fix things. I told one of my city friends that I was installing magnets to hold the cabinets shut. He responded appropriately (for a city friend), "You're so handy; I would never do something like that. I'd hire someone to get it done." Country folks do it themselves. The biggest store in the little town near my church is a Do It Center.

So what is a guy like me to do in a place like this? Find common ground. I'm a city boy, but my mom wasn't. She was raised on a farm. We used to go see Grandpa Tim on the farm when I was growing up. I talk a lot about that farm. I find common ground and lean into it. I'm also learning to fix more than just cabinet magnets, and I make a point of talking about it. And I try not to talk about my GPS.

Finding common ground is not just about the conversation. Go to *their* favorite restaurants. Dress like *they* dress. Find something in common, and lean into it.

In group life, we have a lot of differences. Perhaps you don't have that much in common with some of the people in your group. Find what you do have in common. Ultimately, what we all have in common with our group members is Jesus. And what we have in common through Jesus trumps everything we *don't* have in common!

Talk about your vulnerabilities

There's nothing quite as disarming as talking about your weaknesses and vulnerabilities. Especially if you're a leader, people tend to think you have it all together and don't have any problems. Being appropriately transparent about your struggles in life changes everything.

I made a hospital visit this week and spent quite a bit of time with the family. If you peel back the layers of almost any family and listen long enough, you'll very likely find considerable dysfunction. This family was no exception. In fact, they were feeling a little uncomfortable, like they'd been a little *too* self-disclosing. The relationship was settling into the pretention that I was the holy man who had it all together and they were the folks with the problems.

I then made a point to share about some of my own struggles. I talked about problems—real problems we've dealt with in our own family. You could see the change in their expressions. They felt good to be with a fellow human again—a real human with problems like theirs.

Of course, as in many areas, there's such a thing as too much too soon. Too much information (TMI), as we now like to say. We must find the narrow way. Generally, though, people tend to disclose too little about themselves, not too much. We want people to think well of us. It's better, however, to want them to *know* us.

I once was in a group where a woman talked about her past. She had been a prostitute for a time, and she told us about it. *All* about it. Too much. Too quickly. With too many. It was inappropriate, and we all realized that (except her).

But for every group out of balance in that direction, I've been in 10 that were out of balance the other way. Too stiff. Too impersonal. Too theoretical. Too much about principles and ideas and not enough about real life.

It's a common problem in group life, but it's an easy one to fix. Just be a *little* more self-disclosing yourself.

One more thing: Notice I said "*self*-disclosing," not "my-wife-and-kids-disclosing." As a preacher's kid, I can tell you that being used as every week's illustration gets old. It's sometimes hard to be self-disclosing without giving details that the other people in your life don't want disclosed. Tread carefully. Think about how it's going to affect them. And if you still think it will help others to share about it, get your family's permission first.

Greetings

Did it ever strike you as odd that the Bible tells us how to greet one another? We tend to get lost in the cultural translation, so it's sometimes easy to miss. "Greet one another with a holy kiss" (2 Corinthians 13:12, NIV). The Living Bible puts it in terms we can understand: "Greet each other warmly in the Lord."

Note, however, that it's still a command. We're commanded by God to greet one another appropriately. As surely as God has commanded us to pray or serve or give, God has commanded that we greet one another warmly in the Lord. So what's the big deal?

It's *not* a big deal—as long as you do it. I can be a little spacey and sometimes fail to do this. I've walked right by people and not even noticed or acknowledged they were there. Guess what? I hurt their feelings. I wasn't trying to, but I did. God tells us not to do this. Pull your head out of the clouds and pay attention. These are people with feelings. Look at them. Greet them warmly in the Lord.

I've heard Rick Warren reduce the approach to this formula: a look, a touch, a word. Look the person in the eye, touch the person appropriately (hug from the side), and say a word of encouragement. A look, a touch, a word.

Study the life of Jesus, and you'll find he often treated people this way. He looked at them. He touched them appropriately. He spoke encouraging words to them.

Take some time to evaluate how people are greeted as they enter your group. Make sure everyone is acknowledged and warmly greeted. If you have a larger Sunday-school-type group, consider having greeters at the door as you would before a worship service. This isn't appropriate in every situation, but in a larger group, it might be necessary to be more organized to ensure that everyone's greeted. No matter what size your group is, warmly greeting everyone is vital.

Self-care is *not* selfishness

Philippians 2:4 says, "Each of you should look not only to your own interests, but also to the interests of others" (NIV). In other words, it's OK to look to your own interests; just don't stop there. Self-care, in itself, isn't selfishness. If you take care of yourself, you can serve others better. In the words of the late General George S. Patton Jr., (or so I've heard) "Fatigue makes cowards out of us all."

Imagine two half-full glasses. I pour into you, and you pour into me. I listen to you, and you listen to me. We serve each other, listen to each other, encourage each other. That is how relationships work in an ideal world. In the real world, there is evaporation. Some of what I mean to pour into you doesn't make it in. Over time, both of our glasses become a little less full.

Now, picture a pitcher. That's God. God pours into both of our lives, filling us with his love and grace and acceptance. My glass is full now, so I now have something to pour into you. That's how Christian relationships are supposed to work.

But I must stand under the Pitcher. That's the true meaning of self-care. It's really God-care—we allow God to fill us with his love and grace and acceptance. It also includes following him into the green pastures that he promised to lead us into. Here is one of my favorite verses, and it relates well to this topic: "In vain you get up early and stay up late, eating food earned by hard work; certainly He gives sleep to the one He loves" (Psalms 127:2, HCSB).

Sleep is a practical way we can take care of ourselves. It's one way God refills our cups. A comprehensive list of all the ways we can take care of ourselves falls outside the scope of this book, but for now, walk away with this one thought: Self-care, when we keep God at the forefront, is not selfishness. So take care of yourself so you can take care of others.

Initiate

I love being with people. There are few things I enjoy more than a house full of people on a Friday night. We invite people over, and I love having them over. Occasionally, however, I've heard people complain. Apparently we didn't invite some people quite enough, or some were hurt that we didn't have them over.

It's probably my selfishness, but my first thoughts often go something like this: Have you ever invited *me* over? How many times have you invited *anyone* over? Instead of just waiting at home for the phone to ring, why don't you take some initiative and invite someone yourself? If you're lonely, *do* something about it.

Selfish, I know.

Still, it gets me thinking. For all the times we've done something with friends, how many times did I initiate, and how many times did they? Of all the lunches I've enjoyed, how many times did I set it up, and how many times did someone call me? I'd estimate that I've done 90 percent of the initiating.

I could get pretty depressed about that if I wanted to. Or I can accept that this is reality and that if I don't want to sit home alone every Friday night, I'd better pick up the phone.

Relationships will not come to you. You have to call. You have to e-mail. You have to invite.

Of course, this too can be overdone. Have the good sense to know when you're pestering people. If you ask someone to lunch multiple times and he or she is always busy, back off and see if they invite you.

What do they want to talk about?

My brother is very quiet. He often answers questions with one-sentence answers. And mostly, one-syllable answers. A typical example:

"How are you doing?"

"Fine?"

"How is church?"

"Good."

"How is Margret doing? I heard she had surgery on her foot."

"Fine. The surgery went fine." (Count 'em: *five* words! Woo-hoo!)

"How's the weather been?"

"Cold."

And on it goes, until you get him on a topic he's interested in. Get him talking about worship, and a flaming evangelist erupts. Like a lot of us, he's had a string of hobbies. The current one is motorcycle riding, although by the time you read this, he'll likely be on to something else. Get him on the topic of his current hobby and *vroom!* The conversation is off and running faster than a Yamaha guy at a Harley-Davidson convention.

My brother recently rode from Colorado Springs up through the Rockies, through Yellowstone and Glacier National Park and into Canada. Eleven days by himself on his motorcycle. No one to talk to; no one to listen to. He slept in a tent. This sounds awful to me. My idea of camping is "Camp Marriott." I get tired of listening to myself *think* after three days. But ask Rick about his trip to Canada, and he'll erupt with exuberant, enthusiastic conversation.

Most people have some hot buttons. Find them.

Someone overheard me talking to a woman at church the other day. "Wow, she was sure in a talkative mood," he said. "I've never heard her say two words to anyone!"

"Ever ask her about her horses?"

"Oh yeah, I knew she did horses, but that's not so interesting to me, so I never talk about that."

If you want to win with people, talk about what *they* want to talk about. Talk about *their* interests, *their* hobbies, *their* sports, *their* kids. Most people love talking about their kids or grandkids, if they have any. If you're in someone's home, look around the room. Look for photos on the wall, and notice the boat or camper outside. Ask about them. Once you get onto that hot spot, you will hardly be able to shut them up.

A gentle answer—not a *right* answer

"A gentle answer turns away wrath, but harsh words cause quarrels" (Proverbs 15:1, TLB). Notice it says a *gentle* answer, not a *right* answer. The tone of your voice has as much to do with your success with people as anything I know. This is especially true in tense situations. You can say almost anything and get away with it if you use the right tone.

This story still sticks in my craw: I stopped to get gas at a Sam's Club a few months back. My gas tank fills from the passenger's side, but all the pumps on that side were full and had long lines. The ones on the other side were open. So I flipped a quick U-turn and came in the other way. The Gas Pump Nazi, in charge of overseeing the pumps, did not like this one bit. This was his kingdom, and he wanted everyone to play by the rules. I wish I could demonstrate his body language. He came running from his throne waving his hands and screaming. "Turn around! You can't come in this way! You must go the other way!"

I did retail for a time. The first lesson in retail is that the customer is always right. Our friend apparently didn't attend that school.

I was pretty calm at this point. "Sir, it's a long wait going the other way. There is no one going this way. You don't want me to go to your competitor, do you?" I smiled as I spoke.

"I don't care where you go, but you are not going this way!"

I was shocked that he would go to the mat and give up a sale over which way people drove through the bays. I'd bet he wouldn't think that way if he owned the place.

I thought, I don't want to have this conversation. I'm just going to get a little gas and go on my way. I went to grab the pump.

He screamed, "You can't do that!"

I'm thinking, "Watch me. Who's bigger?" (Thinking, not saying, mind you.) He started screaming, running the other way. "I will hit the emergency switch and shut down the whole place."

Wow, I thought, he's really dialed up about driving the right direction. At this point I started to imagine all the other customers looking at me angrily, so I let it go. I drove to his competitor and got some gas there.

Don't miss the point of this story. I would have complied gladly if this gentlemen had come to me with a good tone and said, "Say, I know this is a real inconvenience. I know there's a long line for you going that way and there are no cars going this way, and it makes a lot of sense to do what you've done. I'd probably do the same thing. But my boss is really particular about this. If he were to come out here and see cars going the wrong way, he'd have my hide. Is there any chance you could pull in the other way?"

Tone is everything. A soft answer—not a right answer.

What hill are you willing to die on?

Some issues are not worth the fight. Or as my daddy used to say, "That hill is not worth dying on." And as 1 Corinthians 6:7b says, "It would be far more honoring to the Lord to let yourselves be cheated" (TLB). Sure, you're right, but does it matter? Let it go!

The Gas Pump Nazi at Sam's Club was willing to die on the hill of making sure everyone entered his kingdom the right way. If it was that important to him, he could have gotten what he wanted by using a gentle answer. Another approach would be to not die on that hill at all. Let it go.

I once heard a story of a church that just could not get this right. *Every* hill was worth dying on. For example, they needed a new roof for the church. Half the church wanted brown shingles, while the other half wanted gray shingles. Certainly an issue worth dying for, don't you think?

The "solution": They did half the roof in gray shingles and half the roof in brown shingles. It was a thoroughly ugly result. At least everyone agreed on *that*.

My dad also used to say, "We don't all do things alike." This song also had a second verse: "We don't all *see* things alike." Variety is the spice of life. Different people do things different ways. It's all good. Sure, you'd do it another way, maybe even a better way. That's OK. It's not you. It's not your deal. We don't all do things alike.

What irritates you about the people in your group? Be honest. What decisions do they make that leave you scratching your head—or shaking it?

But how important is it, really? Can you place it in the file labeled "That hill is not worth dying on"?

You can measure someone's character largely by what it takes to put that person in a bad mood. Think about what sets you off and why. And if it's not a hill worth dying on, let it go.

People skills *are* life skills

The quality of your life is largely dependent on the quality of your relationships. If your relationships are good, you're likely to have a good life. If you struggle with relationships, life is often hard. It's the same with the life of your group.

I have read a lot of theories on how to grow groups, from César Castellanos's G-12 model to David Yonggi Cho's 5x5 cell model, Andy Stanley's closed groups, Larry Osborne's sermon groups, and Nelson Searcy's semester-by-semester groups. We Americans love our models. And we think that if we find just the right model, our groups will grow. And they might—but *only if* our people love each other.

If people learn to get along and develop real community, and learn to love being together, their groups will grow. If people in small groups love each other and get along, their groups will grow. If people in Sunday-school-style groups love each other and get along, *their* groups will grow. The key isn't the model; it's the love people find in the group.

The opposite is also true. Show me a group or a church where there's conflict, bitterness, dissension, and backbiting, and I will show you a group or a church that's not growing. In fact, it's probably falling apart. Even the best model for growth won't help a group or church that's lacking in love.

So how well do you get along with others? How would you evaluate your people skills? If we want our groups—and ourselves—to grow, we would do well to become lifelong learners of people skills. And as we do, we'll become lifelong learners of the people themselves. Which is what Jesus wants from all of us.

spiritual vibrancy— what it is and how to get it

When I drive long distances, I like to get the map out every now and then. Not to see where to turn—I have a GPS that tells me that—but because I want to see the whole trip—where I've been, where I'm going, and where I am now.

We've already gone a long distance in these pages. Therefore, before we go any further, let's get out the map and see where we've been.

We looked at three things that didn't matter all that much:

- Who should get more of your time, outsiders or insiders? Answer: Keep it balanced.
- Do groups have to get the vision first? Answer: No, they don't. They just have to do what's in the vision; when they see it work, *then* they'll catch it.
- Does being a good group organizer help? Answer: Yes, but not as much as you'd think. And the organizer doesn't have to be you.

Then we looked at four things that mattered a little more:

- Should we spend more time on the lesson or more on the group? Again, balanced is best, but err on the side of the group.

- What should we major in—outreach or spiritual growth? Outreach. Because more outreach *leads* to more spiritual growth.
- How important is teaching? The better the teaching, the more likely the growth. But it's usually not the deciding factor. Just make sure you're teaching a halfway decent lesson.
- How much does visitation help? Some, especially if you're good at it. But there are other things that help even more.

Four things matter a lot. We've looked at three of them so far:

- Lots of parties. It sounds too easy to be important, but it's *very* important. Groups with nine or more parties a year are twice as likely to be growing as those groups with four or fewer parties a year.
- High involvement. Don't be a leader with a group; be a facilitator with a team. Groups with high involvement are more than twice as likely to be growing. And if you have lots of people helping with those parties, you're three-and-a-half times more likely to be growing.
- People skills. And strong people skills will not only increase the odds that your group will grow; they'll enhance just about every other area of your life as well.

That's where we've been so far. Now let's move forward. What matters more than anything we've mentioned so far?

Spiritual vibrancy. Leaders who rated themselves high on spiritual vibrancy were nearly three times more likely (182 percent) to have groups that were growing than those who rated themselves low in this area.

I conducted a follow-up survey of group members, asking them the same questions I asked their leaders. The difference was even more pronounced. Groups with leaders described by their own members as having a high spiritual vibrancy were **467 percent** more likely to be growing.

This is great news. But I'll bet you're asking yourself (and me) a question right now: What exactly *is* spiritual vibrancy?

What I mean by spiritual vibrancy is captured pretty early on in the Bible: "And you must love the LORD your God with all your heart, all your soul, and all your strength" (Deuteronomy 6:5). People who are spiritually vibrant are passionate. They're on fire. They're literally on a mission from God, and it shows.

This question, naturally, led to yet another follow-up survey. I asked, "How can we help our groups become spiritually vibrant? What happens in a group that tends to produce spiritually vibrant people?"

I'd like to highlight the four things that I discovered to have the strongest correlation to spiritual vibrancy:

- Feeling loved by the group predicts spiritual vibrancy.
- A positive atmosphere predicts spiritual vibrancy.
- Practical teaching predicts spiritual vibrancy.
- Strong agreement with the statement, "It is always in my best interest to live the Christian life," predicts spiritual vibrancy.

Let's look closer at each of these four ideas and discover how we can create an environment in our groups that's spiritually vibrant.

Love, love, love

Jesus said if we remain in him, we will bear much fruit (John 15:8). He also told us what that abiding looks like. It happens by obeying, and Jesus' most important command was that we love one another. "When you obey my commandments, you remain in my love, just as I obey my Father's commandments and remain in his love….This is my commandment: Love each other in the same way I have loved you" (John 15:10, 12).

Obedience enables us to abide in Jesus, and abiding in Jesus causes us to bear fruit. And the primary command Jesus wants us to obey is to love one another.

We would expect, then, that groups where people feel loved would be fruit-bearing groups and, therefore, growing groups. And that's exactly what the survey confirms. Groups in which people feel loved are *three times* as likely to report the highest levels of spiritual vibrancy.

This suggests another reason why the number of parties we have tends to predict growth (see Chapter 3). The more time people in a group spend together, the better they get to know each other, and the better they get to know each other, the more likely they are to feel loved—and *be* loved. My wife shared with me about how this principle has played out with her own women's group:

> One of the wonderful things in my life is that I love and feel loved by the ladies in my Sunday school class. Not only do I love them, I'm crazy about them, and at the risk of sounding full of myself, I think they're pretty gaga about me, too!
>
> The thing is, I haven't always felt that way. Same ladies over the past few years, but very different feelings. I have been a part of this class for four years, but it took close to two years before I felt a close bond with most of them. You want to know what made the difference between just being a part of something and feeling community? feeling like a family? Spending time with them.
>
> And it's not *just* spending time with them that made the difference. It is what we talk about and share during that time that builds that "girlfriend" kind of love. It all started when someone in our group had a wonderful idea. The idea went like this: "Let's all get together for lunch this month and bring a gift for all the gals who have birthdays during this month." We all liked the idea and showed up for lunch—I think there were eight of us. We've been doing it ever since.
>
> During those times together, we've found out that one of our friends lost two husbands in tragic accidents; we've prayed with one of our pals whose son was in a horrible accident while serving in the military—and that same friend lost her mother, who she was very close to. We prayed for her and were sad with her. Our group truly knows what it means to bear one another's burdens. One in our group has grown children who haven't spoken to her in years. All of us who are mothers (and not all of us are) grieve with her and do our best to be there for her as friends who understand. This same friend just lost her sister after taking care of her during her last days. We've had financial struggles, job changes, and sickness, but we've also had celebrations and happy times to share. There is

nothing like cheering with friends when they or someone in their family has experienced victory. When you've been praying for them, it's your victory, too!

For me, it's pretty easy to figure out. You want to love and be loved by those in your small group? Make spending time with them a priority. I know you are busy; so am I. But you'll figure out a way to make it happen if you really want to. I guarantee it is an investment worth making. You'll grow to love 'em and think they're "all that." Who knows? They might just think the same of you!

Spiritually vibrant people are grown in groups of people who feel loved by one another.

Keep it positive

People tend to catch spiritual vibrancy in an atmosphere that's positive and uplifting. An atmosphere that's gloom-and-doom and negative—or filled with ought-tos, you'd-betters, don't-forgets, and shame-on-yous— does *not* tend to create spiritually vibrant people.

People who strongly agreed with the statement, "The atmosphere in my group is positive and uplifting" were more than twice as likely (125 percent) to be at the highest level of spiritual vibrancy, compared with those who only moderately agreed with the statement. You can imagine how it goes from there (and if not, see the Appendix at the end of this book).

So how can we create a biblical, balanced, hopeful, faith-filled atmosphere that's positive, uplifting, and true to the Bible? I can think of four statements that should permeate our teaching and our group atmosphere. If your group would create spiritually vibrant people, return to these themes often.

We are loved, even though we are sinners. Here's another jump-ball question: Does the Bible teach a high view of man or a low view of man? Is our problem that we think too highly of ourselves or that we think too little of ourselves?

From one perspective the Bible teaches a very low view. We're all sinners. The best we can do—our righteousness—is like "filthy rags" (Isaiah 64:6). We do well to humble ourselves before an exalted God. A lot of old hymns speak of this perspective, with lines including "such a worm as I" or "a wretch like me."

On the other hand, as the hymn "Jesus Loves the Little Children" puts it, "Red and yellow, black and white, all are precious in His sight." We are so precious that God gave us his Son. If I gave the life of my son so I could be close to you, I'd feel pretty frustrated (or worse) if you didn't feel loved.

One of my favorite passages on this subject is from Zephaniah: "For the Lord your God is living among you. He is a mighty savior. He will take delight in you with gladness. With his love, he will calm all your fears. He will rejoice over you with joyful songs" (Zephaniah 3:17). God takes great delight in you. He sings over you like a mother singing lullabies over her beloved child.

I did a sermon once on one word. It was a messy, meandering message. It didn't have a lot of structure, no three points and a prayer. Just one point: You are God's beloved. God adores you. God loves you. God *likes* you. God *wants* to hang out with you. I read several Scripture passages that used the word *beloved* and tried to explain the context. No brilliant insights from the Greek, just paraphrasing what's obvious from any English translation. The message wandered back and forth from the stories in the Bible to application to today's life.

At one point, I said, "Maybe there's someone here who doesn't feel loved. You don't feel special. You don't feel treasured. I want to stand before you as God's spokesman and ask you to repent. Repent of not feeling loved. Embrace your status before God as loved by God. Embrace your status as his treasure, the apple of his eye. Embrace the view of yourself that *God* has of you." The message wandered on like this for half an hour. I think my preaching professor would have flunked me.

And yet it was the most complimented sermon I've ever preached. As I reflected on the unexpected result, I came to realize that I'd probably spent too much time preaching and teaching, telling people what they ought to do and should have done, and not enough time telling them they're God's beloved.

At the same time, you wouldn't have to hear me preach very many times before you heard one of my favorite words: *balance*. If the "beloved" message is all you ever teach, you're not teaching the whole counsel of God. Be sure to teach all of God's truth. But don't forget this truth: God loves us. He really, truly does.

Good groups don't only teach this message; they live it. They don't stop with teaching that God loves us; they represent God in loving one another.

We can do better, even though we've failed. A positive, uplifting atmosphere means we're loved. It also means that we can do better. Not just that we *should* do better, but that with God's help we *can* and *will* do better.

We can beat worry. We can get out of debt. We can develop the discipline we need to faithfully spend time in the Word and prayer. We can live healthier lives. We can restore relationships. We can double our classes and grow our churches. We can do all things through Christ who strengthens us.

Too often, group talk is just the opposite. It's not positive and uplifting, nor is it hope-filled and faith-filled. It's "Poor me," "We're just a bunch of dirty rotten sinners," "The world will never be any better, and we just have to learn to live with it." Who wants to come to a group to talk about *that*? How does *that* create spiritually vibrant people?

It doesn't. Spiritually vibrant people are created in an atmosphere that's positive and uplifting. This isn't to say that we can be perfect—only that we *can* do better. We can make substantial improvement. We can be significantly more loving, noticeably joyful, visibly at peace. Jesus really can, and wants to, make that kind of difference in our lives. It is real. It is significant. And it is visible to everyone else in the room. And when that kind of spiritual vibrancy is visible, others catch it.

When I was growing up in the Philippines, I knew a man who was, by his own admission, a very bad man. His name was Mr. Gepte. He had two wives and 24 children and was mean as a snake. He used to cut people with razor blades just for kicks. You didn't want to be his enemy. But Mr. Gepte came to know Jesus.

My dad said, "I can't defend this biblically, but it seems to me that some people get saved and some people get *really* saved." Mr. Gepte got "*really* saved." He visited his son shortly after he came to Jesus, and his son could immediately see the difference. The son said, "My Poppa has a new man inside." He had never heard of 2 Corinthians 5:17 ("If anyone is in Christ, he is a new creation"), but he observed that his daddy had a new man inside.

And this wasn't a flash in the pan. My dad later trained Mr. Gepte's sons and grandsons in Bible school. The prayer of his life was that all of his 24 children would come to Christ. My parents visited Mr. Gepte on his deathbed. And they were able to rejoice with him that God had answered his prayer. All 24 of Mr. Gepte's children had come to know the Lord.

Mean men can get a new man inside. We really *can* change.

Again, growing groups don't just believe this. They *help* one another get better. I had a friend who was struggling to read her Bible every day. She was in college at the time and tended to stay out late, and she struggled to fit quiet time in her schedule. My friend's group leader got in the habit of stopping by her dorm room to wake her each morning. That's just one simple example of how group members can help one another do better.

Romans 8:28 is still true. Life is hard. Sooner or later, we all realize it. People told me as I was growing up that life would be hard, and I got the idea there were speed bumps in life. But I'm not talking about speed bumps. I'm talking about train wrecks. Sooner or later, most of us have them. A divorce, the death of a child, the untimely loss of a husband. Sooner or later, it happens to most of us.

Life can be really, *really* hard. But Romans 8:28 is still true: "And we know that God causes everything to work together for the good of those who love God and are called according to his purpose for them." He can take Joni Eareckson Tada, a quadriplegic, and give her a worldwide platform. He can take Chuck Colson's jail sentence and turn it into an international prison ministry. He can take the pain of your life and bring good from it.

Which brings us to…

God is God. That is it. That is enough. I did a fascinating study of Hebrews 11 a few years back. You know the passage—the famous "faith chapter." It's an encouraging chapter, isn't it? One sound bite after another of people who conquered and overcame through faith.

Then the writer turns a corner. See if you can spot it.

"By faith these people overthrew kingdoms, ruled with justice, and received what God had promised them. They shut the mouths of lions, quenched the flames of fire, and escaped death by the edge of the sword. Their weakness was turned to strength. They became strong in battle and put whole armies to flight. Women received their loved ones back again from death.

"But others were tortured, refusing to turn from God in order to be set free. They placed their hope in a better life after the resurrection. Some were jeered at, and their backs were cut open with whips. Others were chained in prisons. Some died by stoning, some were sawed in half, and others were killed with the sword. Some went about wearing skins of sheep and goats, destitute and oppressed and mistreated. They were too good for this world, wandering over deserts and mountains, hiding in caves and holes in the ground" (Hebrews 11:33-38).

Here's my take-away from this passage: We cannot be certain that God will answer any particular prayer the way we asked him to, except when we pray for the forgiveness of sins. Sometimes God says yes. Sometimes God says no. And sometimes God says "Wait." Sometimes we pray that God would take this thorn from our flesh, and God responds only with "My grace is all you need. My power works best in weakness" (2 Corinthians 12:9). Jesus prayed, "Let this cup of suffering be taken away from me" (Matthew 26:39). God didn't take it away. Faith isn't being certain that God will positively answer any particular prayer. It's knowing that his answer will be what's best.

God is God. That is it. That is enough. We can't be sure God will do this or fix that. We can't be sure that God will do *any* particular thing. We *can* be sure that he is God. God is good. God is wise. God knows all things. God loves us. God's ways are higher than our ways. At times, we may not like the way God runs the universe, and we may not like the way he runs the circumstances of our lives at times. But God's way is *always* the better way.

Pastor Kenton Beshore is fond of talking about "double-fisted faith" and uses the following passage to do it:

"Shadrach, Meshach, and Abednego replied, 'O Nebuchadnezzar, we do not need to defend ourselves before you. If we are thrown into the blazing furnace, the God whom we serve is able to save us. He will rescue us from your power, Your Majesty. But even if he doesn't, we want to make it clear to you, Your Majesty, that we will never serve your gods or worship the gold statue you have set up' " (Daniel 3:16-18).

Kenton illustrates this passage by holding up one hand and saying, "God will deliver us, but even if he does not"—and here, he holds up the other hand—"we believe that God is God, and that is enough." That is double-fisted faith. We believe God can heal, but even if he does not, we still believe that God is God and that is enough for us. We believe that God can, but even if he does not…

God is God. That is it. That is enough.

So before moving on, let's recap. Spiritually vibrant people are formed and continue to grow in an atmosphere where the following are discussed—often:

- We are loved, even though we are sinners.
- We can do better, even though we have failed.
- Romans 8:28 is still true. God *does* work all things for good for those who love him.
- God is God. That is it. That is enough.

Spiritually vibrant leaders of spiritually vibrant people don't just talk about these things—they talk about them *practically*. They talk about how each lesson applies to their lives. And they *live* their teaching. And that's the subject of our next section.

"What do we *do* with this?"

I was watching the clock in Sunday school. In this case, I was just a member of the class. It was about five minutes to quitting time. The conversation was interesting—even spirited—but I wasn't sure exactly where we were going. So I raised my hand.

"In about five minutes, we're all going to be walking out that door. What exactly do you want us to do about what we heard today?"

Aren't you glad I don't attend *your* group?

That line got to be the running joke in class for months to come. Whenever the conversation got the least bit off subject, our teacher would say, "We need to get back on topic, because I know what Josh is thinking: When we walk out that door, what do you want us to do about what we heard today?"

The truth is, every one of your group members is thinking the same thing. Every week. All the time. They may not say it. They may not be as frank as I am (and my middle name *is* Frank). But they *are* thinking, What am I supposed to do with what we learned today? Every teacher, every week, ought to provide a clear answer to that question.

Practical teaching matters. It was the second most likely predictor of spiritual vibrancy. When lessons focused on application, groups were 125 percent more likely to be highly spiritually vibrant, compared to those whose teaching was only somewhat practical. Practical teaching, more times than not, produces spiritually vibrant people.

In some circles, practical, application-based teaching is contrasted with "deep teaching." Deep teaching is spiritual and theological, and…well, *deep*. Practical teaching is seen as light and fluffy, shallow, and human-centered. In "deep" circles, how-to preaching and teaching don't get a lot of respect.

Here's the problem with that: How-to teaching is what Jesus did. Here's one of my favorite examples. See if you can find the omission in this rendering of the Great Commission:

"Then Jesus came to them and said, 'Therefore, go and make disciples of all the nations, baptizing them in the name of the Father and the Son and the Holy Spirit. Teach these new disciples all the commands I have given you. And be sure of this: I am with you always, even to the end of the age' " (Matthew 28:19-20).

Did you find it?

Let me quote it again, correctly. See if you find the difference.

"Then Jesus came to them and said, 'Therefore, go and make disciples of all the nations, baptizing them in the name of the Father and the Son and the Holy Spirit. Teach these new disciples to obey all the commands I have given you. And be sure of this: I am with you always, even to the end of the age.' "

Find it? It's in verse 20: "Teach them *to obey*." The difference is crucial. Howard Hendricks used to say, "We are not out to make smarter sinners, but saints." It is not to turn out people who can quote the facts of the Bible but live like the devil. It is to teach people to act like saints. We are out to make people a little more loving, a little more joyful, a little kinder, a little more at peace, a little less anxious, a little less angry, a little more like Jesus.

Practical teaching is not an add-on. Application is the *purpose* of teaching. We are to teach people how to—how to pray, how to know their spiritual gifts, how to serve, how to be a good dad or mom, how to give, how to control their tongues, how to beat bad habits. How to live the life.

On that note, let's talk about "how to" teach practical, life-changing lessons. Here are a few tips to get you started:

Good application comes from good doctrine. Don't be intimidated by this. The fact is, there's nothing more practical than clear-headed thinking about theology. We all have a theology, a set of beliefs about God; our beliefs might as well be the *right* beliefs. The book of Ephesians is a great example of combining solid doctrine with application—Chapters 1-3 cover the theology; Chapters 4-6 move on to the practical application of that theology.

As I've said, we need how-to in our lessons. It's something that's all too absent from a lot of teaching in small groups and Sunday schools today. But if you want to build people of faith, confidence, optimism, and high self-esteem, don't *start* with how-to. Start with good theology. Show people what's worth believing about God; then show them how to live it out.

Talk about how God is all-loving and unconditionally accepting. Talk about the fact that we're sinners and that God loves us and wants to deliver us *from* that sin. Once we know those truths, we can move on to applying those truths to our lives.

If we want to help people with their finances, we don't start by teaching them how to buy financial software. We start with God. We first teach that

God owns everything and has made us to be stewards of the things he's given us. We talk about how the purpose of money—and of everything else God gives us—is to glorify God. We talk about what the Bible says about the poor. We talk about giving. Then, when the foundation is laid, we move on to practical, how-to steps of managing money.

Likewise, if you want to teach people about service, don't start with a spiritual-gifts test. Talk about how God is a worker. Jesus said, "My Father is always working, and so am I" (John 5:17). Work is good. Work predates the fall. It was intended not to be a punishment, but to give us purpose. Then introduce the idea that when we're working near the sweet spot of our gifting, we find fulfillment and joy in life. Lay the theological foundation, and *then* get practical.

Always end with "so what?" Remember these three letters: YBH (Yes, but how?) Remember my question: What do you want us to do about what we heard today?

The opposite approach can also work. Start with a life question and, before you go to application, ask, "What does the Bible have to say about this?" And then give biblical answers.

Good teaching is about connecting the Bible to life. It needs to have both the Bible *and* life. You can start with the Bible or you can start with life, but be sure you connect the two.

Distinguish what you *could* do from what you're *going* to do. It's helpful to make this distinction up front. People are then free to think of multiple ideas that might help your group members apply the Word and then later on release those ideas they don't really intend to pursue. To get started, try questions and activities like these:

- What are 10 ways a husband *could* serve his wife?
- Let's go around the room; each person state one way we could reduce worry by 50 percent.
- Let's divide into two teams. We'll see which team can, in two minutes, come up with the most creative ways we could be involved in faith-sharing.

Emphasize in this first phase, that the group isn't committing to anything yet—you're just brainstorming things you *could* do. There are no bad ideas in brainstorming; it simply frees people's minds and hearts to be creative and to bring up ideas in an environment where they're not going to be acted on immediately—or shot down.

Once you've gotten a variety of ideas, *then* go for the sale: What are you going to do? What do you want to do about what we talked about today?

This application can take one of two forms—baby steps or the big order. Oftentimes, the best way to do application is to ask for baby steps. Sometimes we ask people to live holy and godly lives and they can't figure out how to get to square one.

The Navigators have a little booklet titled *7 Minutes With God*. The point of it isn't to limit your time with God to seven minutes, but to make quiet time doable. Who can't set the alarm seven minutes early? It's a baby step. Anyone can do it. Once you get there, you might have so much fun that you want to do more. But if a leader asked for an hour of prayer up front, it might be so overwhelming that you'd end up doing nothing. Sometimes we do well to ask for baby steps.

Sometimes, however, we would do well to go way beyond baby steps. Sometimes we need to challenge the group to lay down their lives and follow Christ. Sometimes we need to ask them to quit being halfhearted. Sometimes we need to ask for a commitment that's going to stretch people past their comfort zones. Sometimes we need to ask for the big order. There's a time and a place to step up and commit to something so big that you *can't* do it without totally relying on God.

Often we need to ask for baby steps first; eventually we need to ask for the big order. We have not because we ask not.

One more thing characterizes groups of spiritually vibrant people.

Loving the Christian life

I've written thousands of sentences, but I've written only one that I think is profound. And I've discovered that strong agreement with this statement predicts spiritual vibrancy. Here it is.

We must come to *love* the Christian life, or we will never come to *live* the Christian life.

Let me give just a few examples of what I mean:

- We must come to love prayer, or we won't pray very well. If prayer is a duty and an obligation rather than a delight, we're probably not praying very well.
- We come to love serving, or we're not serving very much. Or at least, not serving much in love. If we're going to stay with it, we'll have to come to love it.
- We come to love the Word, or we struggle to spend time in the Word.

So let me repeat: **We must come to *love* the Christian life, or we will never come to *live* the Christian life.**

Self-discipline can get overrated in a lot of Christian teaching. Not to say that there isn't a place for self-discipline. Sometimes we need to do what needs to be done, whether we feel like it or not. But if you try to live your entire life this way, you're probably in trouble. Or at least miserable. If you spend your whole life forcing yourself to do what you really don't want to do, you'll run out of steam. Eventually you'll do what you believe to be in *your* best interest, even if it means abandoning what really *is* in your best interest.

You must come to *love* the Christian life, or you will never come to *live* the Christian life.

I put this statement to the test—or rather, to the survey—and it passed with flying colors. In fact, this single factor affected spiritual vibrancy more than anything else I could find. People who *strongly* agreed with the statement, "It is always in my best interest to live the Christian life," were 145 percent more likely to be spiritually vibrant when compared with those who only moderately agreed. And when compared with those who were neutral or who disagreed, those who strongly agreed were **350 percent** more likely to be spiritually vibrant.

We are irrevocably hard-wired to pursue what we believe is in our best interest. We can't avoid it. Therefore, if we truly believe that we'll find our greatest reward in following God, Jesus' yoke becomes easy. We follow him almost automatically. If, on the other hand, we think we should follow Jesus but would rather go our own way, we're going to be in a constant battle of the will with ourselves.

It's not enough to submit our will to God. Merely believing that God exists isn't enough. We need to believe that his life is the most rewarding life imaginable. We must believe that it's impossible to follow Jesus and not be rewarded. Ought-to, should, and you'd-better will never do. We must believe that following Jesus is the most rewarding life that exists.

In the last chapter, I mentioned how much I enjoy what I call jump-ball questions. Here's another one: "Should you serve God to give or to get?" Try it on your group sometime, and see what kinds of responses you get.

Here's my take, courtesy of Hebrews 11:6: "And without faith it is impossible to please God, because anyone who comes to him must believe that he exists and that he rewards those who earnestly seek him."

We must believe that God exists. That part's pretty easy; about 95 percent of the people in the world claim they believe God exists. Even the demons believe God exists (James 2:19). But we must also believe that God *rewards*. If we don't believe that God has good gifts for us, we won't desire God. That's human nature. That's how God built us.

Jesus emphasized this in Mark 10:29-31: " 'Yes,' Jesus replied, 'and I assure you that everyone who has given up house or brothers or sisters or mother or father or children or property, for my sake and for the Good News, will receive now in return a hundred times as many houses, brothers, sisters, mothers, children, and property—along with persecution. And in the world to come that person will have eternal life. But many who are the greatest now will be least important then, and those who seem least important now will be the greatest then.' "

Spiritually vibrant people love God. They love serving God, they love being with God, and they love the rewards God gives them. They not only love serving God, but *like* serving God as well.

How far can you push this?

But is it always in our best interest to live the Christian life? Always? No exceptions?

A lot of people don't want to sell out to God because they're afraid God will call them to missions in the poorest, most dangerous parts of the world. And God might. But do you know what God does to the heart of those he calls to missions? I do, firsthand.

My parents served as missionaries in the Philippines for 25 years. I remember sitting with my mom after breakfast one day. The conversation slowed down, and my mom seemed lost in thought. She looked out the window and then looked back at me. "I think the Philippine people are the prettiest people on planet Earth." That's what God does to the heart of those God calls to missions.

Not that there wasn't a price to pay. When my sister married, my parents couldn't attend the wedding. They were 10,000 miles away. They watched my brother give her away by way of videotape.

By the time my second and third children were born, my parents were retired and able to visit and help out. But they were on the other side of the world when our first child was born. My parents have no memory of Dawson before he was two years old. There is a price to pay for serving God.

My mom lost a brother in a tragic farming accident. She wanted very badly to be at the funeral. But transportation costs were prohibitive, and cost aside, it would have taken too long to get there. There is a price to be paid for serving God.

But my parents wouldn't trade their missionary lives for anything. They're 85 years old now, and they have no regrets. That's how it is when you follow God.

We have to believe it's in your best interest to follow God because we're hard-wired to pursue what we truly believe is in our best interest. Therefore, we won't draw near to God unless we believe he's a rewarder.

You must come to *love* the Christian life, or you will never come to *live* the Christian life.

And sometimes giving up our lives to God literally means giving up our lives *for* God. Perhaps you remember the story of Cassie Bernall. She was a high school student in Littleton, Colorado. She was a good kid who had recently rededicated her life to Jesus and was active in her youth group.

She was in the library, minding her own business, working on a paper. Two of her classmates came in, shooting everyone in sight. She dropped to her knees in a praying position. One of the shooters pointed a gun at her face. The forensic evidence suggests it was touching her face when it went off. Perhaps taking a cue from Cassie's praying position, he asked her a question: "Do you believe in God?"

The biography of Cassie's life, *She Said Yes,* describes that moment in the library. Cassie said yes. And that *yes* cost her her life on earth.[1]

People might be tempted to wonder, Wouldn't she have been better off just to cave? Couldn't she have remained silent or said, "I just don't want any trouble"? More to our point, would Cassie have agreed that we must love the Christian life, even if it costs us our earthly lives?

I think if Cassie could read this, she would say, "Yes, yes, a thousand times yes!" It is *always* in our best interest to live the Christian life, no matter what. We will always be glad we did. It may take a while to fall in love with it. It may only be from the viewpoint of eternity that we see that it was in our best interest. But ultimately, and forever, you'll always be glad you followed Jesus. And forever lasts a long, long time.

There's just one thing left to discuss, and it's the number-one factor in determining what makes groups grow. Let's talk about it now.

section three

what makes groups grow the most

o   MAKE YOUR GROUP GROW

chapter 7

you gotta have faith

The Grand Coulee Dam in Washington state is the largest power-producing facility in the United States, as well as the largest concrete structure—almost a mile long and taller than the Great Pyramid of Giza. It contains enough concrete to build a 60-foot-wide highway, 4 inches thick, from Los Angeles to New York City. Yet all that massive energy-creating power is worthless without a conduit—some means of getting that energy to where it's needed. The closest large city is Spokane, a roughly 2-hour drive. Even enormous power without a conduit to deliver it is of little value.

Likewise, we might have done everything right in our groups. We're throwing parties. We're working as a team. We're connecting with other people. We're even showing a spiritual vibrancy that makes it obvious that we're loving God with all our hearts, minds, souls, and strength. And yet, there's one thing more we need.

Faith.

The correlation is huge. Groups that believe they *will* grow are **nearly 12 times as likely** to be growing, compared with those that don't believe they'll grow.

faith and growth

% OF GROUPS GROWING

80%
70%
60%
50%
40%
30%
20%
10%
0%

Believe the groups will grow   Don't believe the groups will grow

Jesus taught us this would be so. The conduit is not our righteousness or our knowledge, but our faith. Just a few examples: When Jesus healed the blind men, he said, "Because of your faith, it will happen" (Matthew 9:29b); Another time Jesus healed a Roman officer's servant. Jesus said, "Go back home. Because you believed, it has happened." (Matthew 8:13); Jesus also healed a Gentile woman's daughter, saying "Dear woman…your faith is great. Your request is granted." (Matthew 15:28).

In these and other passages, Jesus taught both a profound spiritual reality and a practical way of living. Faith and confidence have a tendency to create their own reality. There's a great deal of research around the idea that confident people tend to do better at almost everything. As the saying goes, "Whether you think you can, or whether you think you cannot, either way you are right."

Of course, we can take this too far.

But, the basic principle Jesus taught us stands. Faith and confidence tend to produce their own reality.

This is also true of groups that grow. Groups that grow expect to grow. We say, "I'll believe it when I see it." Jesus said, "You'll see it when you believe it. And if you don't believe it, you won't see it." Jesus taught that good things happen to those who believe.

The obvious question that arises is this: Did the confidence cause the group to grow? Or did the group believe it would grow because it already *was* growing?

My best guess is yes. It's a circular cause and effect—a self-reinforcing cycle.

It's easy enough to see why a growing group would believe they'd continue to grow. The best predictor of the future is the past. If my group has been growing, it's natural to assume that it will be growing in the future. Likewise, if I haven't been able to grow my group until now, why would I expect it to grow in the future? Past growth creates confidence in future growth.

But I believe the opposite is also true, and I want to show why. A group leader's confidence that a group will grow tends to create its own reality. Faith bears fruit. If we want to grow our group, we would do well to develop the confidence that it *will* grow.

And modern psychology agrees with Jesus. In 1905, Harvard professor William James said, "Belief creates the actual fact." He went on to say, "The greatest revolution of my generation is the discovery that individuals, by changing their inner attitudes of their mind, can change the outer aspects of their lives."[1]

Thinking Christians might argue that this is the world's way of thinking. My response is that Jesus said it long before William James ever did. Group leaders who believe their groups will grow tend to lead growing groups.

What difference does confidence make?

Tim Judge of the University of Florida conducted a landmark study that demonstrates the difference confidence makes. Judge and his colleague Charlice Hurst studied the self-evaluations of 7,660 people. The individuals first answered questions in 1979 when they were 14 to 22 years old. Then they were evaluated again in 2004.

Here's what Judge and Hurst learned: People who were more confident in 1979 ended up making more money in 2004. In fact, their income increased at an entirely different rate than the low-confidence group. Money isn't everything, of course, but it's one of the easiest things to quantify.

The people in the high-confidence group had slightly higher incomes in 1979, making, on average $3,496 more per year than the low-confidence group. As each year went by, the gap widened. By 2004 the high-confidence group was making $12,821 more per year.

Confidence also correlated with strong health. When asked about health problems that interfere with work, people in the low-confidence group reported having three times as many health problems as they had 25 years earlier. No one over 50 is surprised to hear that. But the real shocker was that the high-confidence group actually reported *fewer* health problems than they had 25 years earlier. The confident ones are literally feeling better each year.[2]

The Gallup organization conducted a similar study that suggests that confident people have greater job satisfaction and that that job satisfaction tends to grow over time.

What came first?

It would be nice if I could have surveyed 1,000 teachers on the day they started teaching—before they had or hadn't seen any growth—asked them what they expected, and then checked back a year later to see what had happened. Unfortunately, we don't have that data at this time. All I can say is that growth and positive expectation about growth seem to come together. The issue of cause and effect is sometimes difficult to sort out, as the following example illustrates.

Research indicates that kids with high self-esteem tend to get good grades. Kids with high self-esteem seem to be smarter. For this reason, a great deal of effort has gone toward boosting the self-esteem of students. If we boost the self-esteem, the reasoning goes, we can also boost grades.

Only one problem. Bad grades tend to harm students' self-esteem. Who doesn't feel crummy about themselves when they see a D or an F? I got an e-mail recently from a friend in Georgia who said his school district was doing away with grades altogether so as not to harm the self-esteem of students who were getting bad grades. Now that they're not getting bad grades, the reasoning goes, their self-esteem will rise and they'll get better grades. (Of course, it will be hard to prove this without grades.)

What if we assumed the opposite? What if the assumption was not that kids have good grades because they have high self-esteem, but that they have high self-esteem because they get good grades? Who wouldn't feel good about a big A++ on a test?

We cannot prove that groups that grow believed they would grow *before* they saw growth. But the research strongly suggests it.

Develop faith and confidence

If confidence that our group will grow tends to predict growth, then how do we develop confidence? Here are just a few ideas.

Get some small wins—and celebrate them. Don't expect overnight success. Do celebrate every victory. Every new person who comes to your group is a big win. As the saying goes, nothing succeeds like success. Author John Maxwell talks about the importance of "The Big Mo"—momentum. It is far easier to move a moving object.

Take action. Reading books doesn't grow a class—nope, not even a masterfully written book about how to make your group grow. Action does. There's nothing like "stepping out of the boat" to build your faith. Plan some parties, and invite people who'll probably either turn you down or not show up. Get a team together, and give up some of the control you have over the group. Get going. Watch what happens.

Meditate on God's Word. The Bible says, "So faith comes from hearing, that is, hearing the Good News about Christ" (Romans 10:17). If Paul were a statistician, he would have said, "There is a predictive causal relationship between exposure to the Word and faith." Here are a few verses to start meditating on and internalizing:

- "For I can do everything through Christ, who gives me strength" (Philippians 4:13).
- "And I tell you that you are Peter, and on this rock I will build my church, and the gates of Hades will not overcome it" (Matthew 16:18, NIV).

- "And so he did only a few miracles there because of their unbelief" (Matthew 13:58).
- "Then he touched their eyes and said, 'Because of your faith, it will happen'" (Matthew 9:29).

God said it. So let's know it—and then do it.

Be around people who have grown their groups. Confidence that you can grow your group is as much caught as taught. Do all you can to rub shoulders with leaders of growing groups. One of the reasons I believe so strongly that groups can grow is because *I've* heard so many stories about groups that have grown. Here are just a few.

Paul is a pastor in North Carolina. The church was running about 90 in Sunday school. One class has quadrupled. Several others have doubled. Now their Sunday school program has about 230. They've gone to two services and are about to go to three services and two Sunday schools. Paul told me that a real key to their growth was attitude. The people wanted their church and their groups to grow, believed they could grow, and were willing to do whatever it took to grow.

John Sprinkle is minister of education at First Baptist Church of Indian Trail, in a suburb of Charlotte, North Carolina. When he came on staff 12 years ago, the church had 600 people in Sunday school, with 60 groups. Seems pretty impressive already. But 12 years later, 1,830 people attend Sunday school, in 200 Sunday school classes.

John made a video of a presentation at his church. He began the presentation by asking people from a class he started five years ago to come on the stage. Then he asked the people who came out of that class, then the people who came out of those classes. Soon the whole stage was full of people, all of whom were the result of that original class.

I showed John's video at Sarasota Baptist Church in Florida. A teacher came up to me during the break. "We've seen that kind of growth around here." He pointed to a guy getting coffee. "He came out of my group"—he pointed to a guy at the snack table—"and that guy started a group out of that group." He kept pointing around the room, telling stories of groups that came out of his groups and groups that came out of those groups.

After a while, I stopped him. "Could you tell this story publically?" In a few minutes, he had the microphone in his hand. One by one, he asked all the leaders who had come out of his initial group to come up and stand beside him. Then he asked the leaders who had come out of *those* groups. Before long, there were a dozen people standing on the stage beside him— all leaders of groups who had come out of his group.

The pastor of small groups at Sarasota Baptist Church, Dr. Chad Keck, saw this and thought, "I should make a video, too." And a couple of weeks later, he did. He started with one group that formed another group and another and another. At first a handful of people stood on the stage; soon the stage was filled with people who had come out of one group.

I noticed an interesting detail in this video. The picture kept zooming out, the frame growing wider and wider as more people came onto the stage. Suddenly the zooming stopped. Then the picture suddenly jerked wider still. I think the cameraman was looking for an adjustment on his camera that he hardly ever used. The group on the stage was huge—and all those people came out of one group.

Another inspiring video features Chris Imbach from Jacksonville, Florida, who now has great-great-granddaughter classes. He hosted a leadership team meeting at his house with three of the five people in his group (following the principle of high involvement) and served barbecue meatballs. (Chris says the meatballs were critical.) The leadership team came up with a mission statement and then dreamed a dream about what they wanted to accomplish together over the next 12 months. They were looking for something measurable and something connected to the purpose statement. Then they worked on strategy. Chris had read *You Can Double Your Class in Two Years or Less,* so he decided to employ the party strategy. They communicated the plan, implemented the plan, and evaluated the plan. They got a team together and had some parties, being careful to invite every member and every prospect. They have created seven new "life groups" in the last five years.

I get these kinds of stories all the time. In fact, while writing this chapter, I received the following e-mail from Jody Mazzola, an executive pastor in Plano, Texas:

God's hand of blessing has really been on our young couples' classes. Three years ago, we started serving in a class that had four, sometimes six, people in attendance.

Over these last three years, we have multiplied from one class to three classes. Our attendance has increased from four to six to 60 people. The number increase is great, but each number represents a life. We have seen lives changed for Jesus Christ….

These are some of the steps we have embraced to grow our groups: 1) we believed God wants our classes to grow; 2) also, we have the desire to grow and do what it takes to grow it; 3) a commitment to contacting those on the roster and our prospects by phone, e-mail, and personal visits; 4) we pray, plan, and prepare for Sunday mornings and class events; 5) open our homes for regular fellowships; 6) teach lessons that are applicable to daily living; 7) grow the leadership base. I believe in working myself out of a job.

Chris was baptized two weeks ago. Chris and Sarah were present the very first Sunday our second class started in June. At one of our fellowships over the summer, I noticed Chris and Jeff, the teacher of the new class, sitting on an ice chest talking. As I saw them, I remember praying, asking the Lord to lead in the conversation. Throughout the summer, we loved on Chris and Sarah. With a lot of prayer, love, encouragement, patience, lunches, fellowships, and even tears, Chris received Jesus as his Savior and Lord. Life transformation—*that's* what it's all about!

Believe you can grow

One of the questions I am asked most often goes something like this: "Josh, I know your plan will work. But how do I get my people to *work* the plan?"

We have to lead people to believe that they *can* grow their groups. I may be overly optimistic, but I really think that if your average leader really believed he or she could reach 1,000 people in the next 10 years by growing and reproducing groups, that leader would embrace the vision and work the plan. But most leaders don't believe this is realistic. The challenge is to get them to believe.

The issue of how belief affects the success of an idea has been carefully researched elsewhere. Everett Rogers, in his landmark study reported in *The Diffusion of Innovation,* tracked more than 5,200 independent studies of how ideas spread through a population.[3]

The term *diffusion* was popularized by Bryce Ryan and Neal C. Gross, who published a study in 1943 that became the model for later studies of the diffusion of innovative ideas. Gross interviewed more than 300 farmers to track their use of a new strain of corn that produced 20 percent more yield, was more drought and disease resistant, and worked better with the new mechanical harvesting machines, but that required farmers to buy seed every year from agribusiness companies. The hybrid corn was introduced in 1928, but five years later, only 10 percent of the farmers in the study were using it. Then, suddenly, use of the hybrid corn seeds took off. Based on the interviews, Ryan and Gross plotted an S curve to show the diffusion of the new idea.[4]

I see the dynamic Rogers described in church life all the time. A young guy comes out of seminary all fired up to grow his church. He starts teaching the church how to grow. They don't buy it.

So, the pastor takes matters into his own hands. He takes a class—probably the young married class because he's young and married—and puts his ideas into practice. He's spiritually vibrant, has confidence his class will grow, uses good people skills, plans parties, and gets the whole team involved. The group grows.

"Now," he says to himself, "the church will believe this works." He knows it's all about belief. If they see it and really believe it, everything will change.

They don't.

Well, he thinks, it's because I'm the pastor that they don't believe. If I turn this group over to someone who doesn't work for the church and isn't seminary trained, surely *then* they'll believe it. The pastor turns the group over to one of his group members.

It doesn't help. People still don't believe. They can see it right before their eyes, and they still don't believe. What's going on here?

The biggest finding to come out of Rogers' research was this: The merit of a new idea did not predict its adoption rate. Further, it's not enough to get a few people to adopt the idea and let the rest watch. *You have to get the **right** people to adopt it.*

Rogers' research revealed that the first people to latch onto a new idea are usually not the influencers. Instead, they are the innovators, the think-outside-the-box types, the guys in the Bermuda shorts, the young-married-adult teachers who have only been members of the church for 18 months.

So how do you find out who the people of influence are in your congregation?

Ask.

Ask your people who the five most influential people in the church are. Then make it your aim to get those people on board. Once they're on board, it becomes almost impossible for everyone else not to join in. If your influencers resist, you'll never get the rest of the church to believe. Kerry Patterson, author of *Influencer,* described influencers this way, "They are different from innovators in one critical respect: They are socially *connected* and *respected....* The rest of the population—over 85 percent—will not adopt the new practices *until opinion leaders do.*"[5]

How do you get your influencers to believe in the plan? Well, you could buy all of them a copy of this book. I won't mind. And it might help. But there's a better way.

Experience.

Experience is the holy grail of persuasion and belief. Telling almost never works. Most people are more like Thomas than they'd like to admit. It was when Thomas put his hand in Jesus' side—not a moment sooner—that he believed. Most people are like that. You'll never lead them to believe that it's possible to grow a group by telling them it's possible to grow a group. When they experience it for themselves, however, it will be almost impossible to *dis*believe.

So give your influencers their own success stories. Invite them to some parties, and invite other guests. Include recent visitors to the church and people who have been absent from the group. Don't talk about *why* you're doing it. Don't raise their expectations so they expect someone to join every time there's a party. Just have parties, invite them, and invite potential members. Before six months are up, you'll hear them say, "You know, it seems every time we have someone over they start coming to church."

That moment is the win. Your church is about to change.

Don't pounce on the statement or get overly excited. Say something like, "You know, I think that's a good observation." Trust that these people of influence will tell others who'll tell others. When people of influence talk, other people listen. The church will come to believe as the people of influence come to believe.

In the final two chapters I'll give you a bunch of practical ideas that both pastors and group leaders can adopt or adapt to help others believe—and as they believe, help their groups to grow. But first, I'd like to share one more faith-building tool you can use as soon as you put down this book.

Makeyourgroupgrow.com

Imagine you sat down and had lunch every Sunday with a dozen other teachers, all of whom were growing their groups. Each week you'd hear stories of new people who came, of people who placed their faith in Jesus, of people who rededicated their lives, of parties they had and people they invited, of lives that were being changed. Imagine this happened every week. One week a guy comes in and says, "I now have great-great-granddaughter classes." Another week a guy shares about how his group has grown from 6 to 60 with eight subgroups in the last four years. Week after week after week, you hear these stories. How much do you think that would impact your confidence that you could grow *your* group?

For the past 12 years I've been training leaders to grow groups. And when it happens, they're excited about it. They *want* to talk about it. Leaders will come up to me before or after a conference and ask, "Can I tell you *my* story?"

I've heard hundreds of these stories. You've heard only a small percentage of them here. If you had traveled with me the last 12 years, you would almost certainly share my faith that group leaders can grow groups—

simply on the basis of having heard the stories of so many group leaders who *have* done it. And now that you've traveled 112 pages with me here, hopefully you're beginning to believe it, too.

A couple of years back I started hauling my video camera around with me. So now, when someone starts into a story about how he or she grew a group, I stop and ask, "Do you mind if I record this?" Very often, they'll say, "Sure." Sometimes my host will have worked it out so leaders can share their testimonies of how they've grown their groups.

I made a big point in Chapter 3 about social proof—the idea that we're profoundly influenced by the behavior of others in our world. The application earlier was that as we get not-yet Christians in our group and they get to know us, they're far more likely to become Christians. But the same principle applies to growing your group. If you can be around leaders who are growing their groups, believing that your group can grow as well will feel normal.

In this book, you've read real stories from real people showing how their groups have grown using the principles I've either taught or discovered along the way. And now you can see those stories, too, by visiting makeyourgroupgrow.com. You'll find video testimonies of groups that have grown, articles containing the latest research by myself and others, and a current list of training conferences where you can bring your whole team to be trained to grow.

As you listen to story after story after story, you'll feel something happening to you. It has happened to me as I've had the privilege of listening to hundreds of stories of groups that have grown over the years. You'll come to believe. You'll think, I can do that! I can grow a group! And you can! You can do all things through Christ who strengthens you. You *can* make your group grow.

So now, let's look at some practical ideas you can use to make your groups begin to grow—or to grow even more than you'd previously imagined.

section four

make *your* groups grow!

o   MAKE YOUR GROUP GROW

pastors, lead the way!

imagine a world where the normal thing for the normal group in the normal church under normal circumstances was to grow. Imagine that there was nothing unusual or exceptional about it; growing was expected because *it's what happens all the time.*

Imagine also, in this world, that some group leaders sit down to have lunch and swap stories. A young woman speaks up. She's just started leading a group and is a little nervous. "How do you guys do it?" she asks the more senior leaders. "I want my group to grow, but I'm not sure how to do it."

A gal in her thirties says, "I've grown my group through parties. We have a party every month. I have some ladies who do a great job of putting everything together. There are some guys who do some calling for me. I try to help as well, but preparing the lesson each week keeps me busy, so I try to get as many people involved as I can."

Another man says, "We have a bunch of movie buffs in our group. We have this one guy who has this really cool media room with a huge TV and rockin' sound. We watch movies like two or three times a month. Sometimes they're Christian movies; sometimes they're not. We always make a point to invite people from outside the group. We get to know them, and it makes it easy to invite them to our group later on."

Yet another guy chimes in, "We had a guy join our group recently, and it was all about the softball team. One of the guys in our group knew him from work and knew he was into softball. He started coming, got to know the guys, and the next thing you know he shows up at church."

The conversation goes on and on like this. Imagine that this is the norm. That is my dream, my prayer, the guiding obsession of my life.

But there's something else I know about this dream: We won't get there without pastors. Group leaders don't get there because they read how-to books, including *Make Your Group Grow*. Group leaders are led by pastors. It can become the norm in your church for groups to grow, but it will require leadership on the part of pastors.

Notice, I said, "pastors"—plural. Leading by example needs to be done by *all* of the pastors. Cheerleading is mostly the senior pastor's job. Training and rewarding will most likely be done by the small-group pastor. For other pastors and staff, it's more about leading by example. It's about modeling that the normal thing for the normal Christian is to be in a group and for that group to grow. If pastors don't lead, people don't follow. But the entire pastoral staff should be on board. And if you *don't* have a pastoral staff, make sure your influencers are on board (see Chapter 7).

Let's look at some ideas on how to make that happen in four major areas.

Leading by example

If you're going to grow your church by growing groups, the leaders must embody the vision. And your "lead leader" is your senior pastor. As your senior pastor embodies the vision of small groups, people get it.

My friend Lance Witt was in charge of groups at Rick Warren's Saddleback Church before becoming executive pastor there. He told me that once Rick joined a group, group life skyrocketed churchwide. But just as important as Rick being in a group was Rick talking about his group in his messages. By doing so, he raised the value of group life and made it part of the DNA of church life at Saddleback. People began to think, If it's important for someone as busy as Rick Warren, maybe it should be important to me.

Different pastors will have different visions for their small-group ministries, and that's OK. Andy Stanley, for example, champions closed groups. Once a group gets started, newcomers are directed to a new group, rather than an existing group, through a process called GroupLink.

If you listen to Andy, you'll get the idea that closed groups are the key. He has a persuasive argument that closed groups develop trust, get people to open up over time, and get people closer. But just as great athletes don't always really know what made them great, great churches sometimes don't really know what made them great. I believe the reason groups are working at North Point is not because they're closed. It's because the senior pastor stands up about twice a year in the pulpit and says, "I'm in a group; I want *you* to be in a group."

Dr. Johnny Hunt is another who leads by example. Johnny spoke at my home church last year and shared that he still attends a Sunday school class at his church every week. He has plenty of responsibilities that could provide an adequate excuse for not attending—for instance, serving as president of the Southern Baptist Convention—but he still shows up for Sunday school week in and week out.

His minister of education, Allan Taylor, confirms the importance of leading by example: "How can the pastor champion the cause of Sunday school? I think it starts by his joining and attending a Sunday school class himself. His example will send an unequivocal message to the entire congregation that Sunday school is important around here!"[1]

Thus, in a world where many pundits are proclaiming the death of Sunday school, Dr. Hunt has seen his Sunday school grow and grow. When Johnny came to Woodstock, Georgia, in 1986, Sunday school attendance was 275 and worship attendance was 300. At the time of this writing, those numbers have grown. Sunday school attendance is 5,448 and worship attendance is 6,746—a roughly 2,000 percent increase in both attendances. Johnny knows how to grow groups.

Larry Osborne champions sermon-based groups in his excellent book *Sticky Church*. Groups are encouraged to get together and talk about the pastor. (You might be thinking, "They do that at my church *already!*") At these groups, however, Larry encourages people to discuss how his sermons apply to their lives.[2]

And again, while the idea of sermon-based groups is a good one, I don't think you can attribute North Coast Church's success solely to sermon-based groups. Much of the credit must go to Larry's example, not his specific strategy. Larry is well-known for making sure key leaders are involved. Lay leadership and staff are expected to be participating in small groups.

Nelson Searcy, pastor of The Journey in New York City, believes in semester-by-semester groups, where people meet in groups for a set period of time, adjourn, and then start brand-new groups the following semester. The Journey has more people attending groups than attending worship. But again, I think the success has more to do with the pastor and staff leading by example. In Nelson's words, "When it comes to implementing a successful small groups system, every single person on staff has to be involved, starting at the top."[3]

So let me say this again: Pastors, if you want your groups to grow, get in a group. Here are some more ideas on how to get connected and lead by example:

Make the time—any time. One of the benefits of small groups versus Sunday school–style groups is that it's easier for pastors to participate in small groups. Churches that are most successful at transitioning to a small-group model often cancel either their Sunday night or Wednesday night service. Thus, small groups don't replace Sunday school; instead, they're an alternative to Sunday-night services.

A key point to remember is that a group can meet almost anytime, anywhere. If you can't attend on Sunday morning, pastors, start a men's breakfast group one morning or a couples group one evening. It doesn't even have to be part of an official churchwide program. Just call six friends and say, "Let's do life together."

Associate membership. In many churches, the primary small-group system is still Sunday school. And if the church has simultaneous worship services, it's impossible for the pastor to attend. But a pastor can still be involved in a group. One thing we do routinely in Sunday-school churches, where teachers of preschoolers and children are not able to attend, is something we call associate membership. Associate members are invited to all the parties. If the group has a prayer chain, they participate in it. There's much more to healthy group life than simply attending a meeting, and these associate members participate in every way they can, even though they can't attend on Sunday mornings. Preschool teachers do this all the time; pastors can do it, too.

One logical way to implement this kind of participation would be for the pastor to be an associate member of a group his or her spouse is a member of.

Life Transformation Groups. Neil Cole offers an option, which he calls Life Transformation Groups (or LTGs), that any pastor can be involved in. Groups of two or three individuals meet for accountability and fellowship. When a fourth person wants in, one of the existing members starts a new group with him or her. LTGs go through a brief list of accountability questions, and each person is encouraged to read 25-30 chapters of the Bible each week. (If one person doesn't finish that week, every one reads through it again. It's not punishment—it's reinforcement! Really.) A third component is that group members pray for friends who don't know Jesus. The group can meet anytime, anywhere. For more information on this idea, go to cmaresources.org/article/ltg.

Join a group, and love your group. Consider the pastor who says from the pulpit, "I want to encourage you to be in a group. Everyone needs to be in a group." Imagine also that everyone knows *he's* not in a group and that the worship leader, other staff, and other influencers in the church are not in groups. Sometimes what we do speaks so loudly that people can't be bothered with what we say.

But it's not just about obligation and duty. What really makes the difference is the pastor saying, "I love my group. My favorite night of the week is when I get with them. I think you'll love it, too!" Again, we must come to *love* the Christian life, or we will never come to *live* the Christian life. We must come to love groups, or we will never live group life on an ongoing basis.

Being in a group, and even loving it, isn't enough, though. There are three more big things the pastor and staff need to do—and plenty of little ways you can start doing them.

Cheerleading

Which do you think helps more, the pastor attending a group or the pastor cheerleading group life? I would have thought it was the former, but again I would have been wrong. Churches where the pastor attends a group *are* more likely to be growing, but what really makes the difference is the pastor cheerleading groups. Groups in churches where the pastor regularly promotes and encourages group life are 78 percent more likely to be growing than those where the pastor doesn't regularly promote group life.

So how do you get started? Try any or all of these ideas:

Start from the pulpit. If you're going to receive a compliment, wouldn't you rather receive it with a few hundred friends present? So would most of your leaders. The pulpit is a great place to cheerlead what you want to see done. Take stories of groups doing well and work them into your sermons. Catch your leaders doing something right, and tell the rest of your congregation so they can catch it, too.

Put it in print. Many pastors write a regular article for their church's newsletter (or its online cousin, the blog). What a great place to mention the positive achievements of groups! There's something about seeing your name in print that makes an impression. I knew a pastor in Fort Worth, Texas, who did this. His articles were filled with the recognition of people in his congregation who had done well. Lots of them. It was "music to their eyes."

Shoot out an e-mail. All cheerleading doesn't have to be public. I wrote one of my teachers a short e-mail this morning to tell him he did an especially good job with the lesson on Sunday. A small thing, but it keeps the fire hot.

Pick up the phone! Here's one from the old-fashioned technology book: Call your leaders. It doesn't need to be a long call. Just pick up the phone and say, "I know you had an awkward situation in your group. You handled it with great skill. I just wanted to say thank you for all you do and how well you do it." It's guaranteed to make your leaders smile—and to keep at it.

Handwritten=personal. Here's an even more old-fashioned idea: Write a note or send a card. Make it easy on yourself and keep a stack of cards in your desk. When's the last time you got anything in your mailbox that wasn't a bill or junk mail? Sometimes old-fashioned *is* better.

Caffeinated affirmation. I went on Facebook to ask for practical cheerleading ideas. My favorite idea came from Christian comedian Peter Wolf of Fort Worth, Texas: He suggested meetings at Starbucks—and the pastor buys!

If Momma's happy… Sometimes one of the best ways to cheerlead is indirectly. Brag to the leader's wife or husband. He or she is almost certain to pass your words on. And your leader will glow, thinking, My pastor said *that* about *me*?

Make cheerleading automatic and easy. Keep the cards and stamps in your desk. Have all your leaders' numbers in your cell phone. You have all their e-mail addresses in your address book, don't you? Make sure they're all friends on Facebook. Block off a specific time in the week to do cheerleading.

I used to carry a small recording device with me on Sundays. When I saw someone doing something I wanted to encourage, I'd make a brief audio note to myself. Then on Monday, I'd take appropriate action—send a note, write an e-mail, make a phone call, or buy a gift.

Celebrate milestones. Sometimes a delayed reaction is better. Make a note on your calendar at the six-month anniversary of a new group. On that day, write the teacher and say, "I'm remembering it was six months ago today you launched your new group. I know it was a challenge for you. It was a courageous move, but it's paying off. Thanks for all you do." Timing makes a difference. Put it on your calendar, and write the note six months to the day.

Point out the fruit. Cheerlead spiritual progress as well as numerical growth and outward activities. Tell your leaders how you see God working in their lives. Tell them you can see them becoming a little more loving, a little more joyful, a little kinder—a little more "fruity." Telling them can come in any of the forms we've already discussed—public, private, verbal, e-mail, direct, indirect—whatever works best for you and your leader.

Block out time for cheerleading. It doesn't take a lot of time to be a cheerleader, but if you don't make the time, it has a habit of slipping away. Block out half an hour to an hour each week to write the notes, send the e-mails, and make the phone calls.

Every now and then, pull out the stops. Get the most creative, imaginative people in the room to plan a big shindig with decorations, food, music, PowerPoint, video, gifts—whatever you can think of that will encourage your leaders. Most cheerleading is made up of simple, behind-the-scenes things. But every now and then, bring in the marching band.

Training

Training is something else pastors can do to help their groups grow. What do teachers most need to be trained in? Focus on predictors of growth. Here again is the list of big-ticket items we've covered in this book:

- Faith and confidence
- Spiritual vibrancy
- People skills
- Team-building skills
- Hospitality skills
- Outreach strategies (visitation, hospitality, life-style evangelism, or other)
- Teaching skills

My friend Dr. Steve Parr has done a great deal of research on the Baptist churches in Georgia. He points out that two-thirds of Southern Baptist Sunday schools aren't growing, while a third are. What makes the difference? In his study of the 50 fastest growing churches in Georgia, Steve found that all but one of those churches reported that they had a systematic approach to leader training.[4]

Yet my experience informs me that most churches don't do a lot of training. There's a good reason why many of our churches aren't doing well. They don't know *how* to do well. We don't train them.

This is an area, however, where balance and creativity are in order. People are busy. So how can we approach training in a way that equips leaders without overloading them even further? Here are some ideas from leaders both well known and not-so-well known (but who have great ideas nonetheless):

Be creative with your time. Larry Osborne, in *Sticky Church,* says that the biggest mistake North Coast Church made in its early days was to overtrain. They wanted their small-group leaders to be the best-trained leaders anywhere. While that sounds good on the surface, their people had lives. North Coast had to learn how to get creative.

North Coast still has a fall training event, but it's an evening event instead of an all-day event. Group leaders receive CDs to listen to so they can get training on the run—while driving or doing dishes or, well, running. Perhaps North Coast's most creative idea was to do training Sunday morning, during the worship service. While Larry is preaching in one room, the teachers are in another room being trained. I've talked to a number of churches that do this on an annual basis, and they all report the same thing—if they offer training on a Friday night or Saturday morning, they're lucky to get half their leaders there. When they do it Sunday morning, pretty much everyone shows up.

Train on the go. Much of North Coast's training at this point is need-based. So now, when a leader runs into a bump, trainers develop a resource to help the leader work through it or provide coaching to deal with it.[5] Training is done more on a need-to-know basis, because the groundwork has already been laid.

Less is more. Don't hit your leaders with everything. Narrow the scope of their training. Say more about what's really important to them, but don't overload your leaders with more information than they can process. Nelson Searcy agrees with this less-is-more approach. "We've found that a shorter training session can actually be significantly more effective than a longer session."[6] The Journey does half-day training sessions at the beginning of each semester and supplements that with electronic training during the week.

Pool your resources. Training is often done best in cooperation with other churches. Training is the core business of many denominational entities, which are able to provide training that the local church, particularly small local churches, often can't. Bob Mayfield, of the Baptist General Convention of Oklahoma, is one example of a denominational servant who's using cutting-edge technology to train churches today. At Bob's invitation, Ed Stetzer led a live training session at Falls Creek in the summer of 2009. The session was videotaped and made a part of a larger training strategy that included 26 other sessions by other trainers. From there, they were able to create an affordable package that included video as well as a training outline, listening guide, handouts, and PowerPoint presentation.

Megachurches, which operate like mini-denominations, can provide excellent training that your church can take advantage of.

Go high-tech. Technology is helping to make training easier, more accessible, more specific, and more affordable. Webinars, podcasts, and online training are all examples of how technology is making training easier. One great example of online training is missionohio.e-quip.net. The site includes video training for small groups, as well as a number of other church-related topics including leadership, evangelism, and church planting. The site also provides the ability to take notes, which can by saved with your profile, as well as MP3 files for download.

Likewise, Bill Donahue of Willow Creek Community Church (willowcreek.com/grouplife) serves the greater church by providing excellent small-group training via satellite. Churches of almost any size can sign up to be a host.

The technology is out there. Take advantage of it.

Don't write it all yourself. Here is just a small selection of resources you might use with your leaders:

- *Experiencing God,* by Henry Blackaby (B&H Books). This book has stirred my heart in a profound way, as it has for countless others. It's almost certain to cultivate the spiritual vibrancy of the people in your group. *Experiencing God* reminds us that God is always at work all around us, and he calls us to join him in what he's already doing.

- *Desiring God,* by John Piper (Multnomah), is another classic. I quote Piper all the time in my lessons because I want people to get his message. Piper teaches that God is most glorified in us when we are most satisfied in him. God calls us to enjoy him. We must come to *love* the Christian life, or we will never come to *live* the Christian life. Remember? Piper captures this idea and brilliantly expands on it for an entire book. Christianity is not merely about obligation and duty; it's about delighting in God.

- *Why Nobody Learns Much of Anything at Church Anymore (and How to Fix It),* by Group founder Thom Schultz and his wife and chief creative officer, Joani Schultz (Group). At the risk of sucking up, this is a great book! I read it long before I had a book published with Group and can recommend it without hesitation. So how *do* we fix it? The short version: Get *everyone* involved in the learning process, and get them involved in every way possible: touching, smelling, throwing, arguing, tasting, thinking, feeling. Active learners are better learners.

And as we're already discussing Group products, here are two more:

- *Small Group Ministry in the 21st Century: The Encyclopedia of Practical Ideas.* The title says it all. Within the pages of this resource, you'll find more than 600 ideas including icebreakers, approaches to group prayer, ways to welcome new members and get everyone more involved, movie nights, questions to deepen group relationships, creative approaches to Bible study, worship ideas, and ideas about how to serve your community. And much more.

- *R.E.A.L.: Surprisingly Simple Ideas for Adults.* This one boils Group's proven approach to adult learning down to an easy-to-use pocket guide. The R.E.A.L. approach includes simple strategies that help you take what you're *already* doing in your lessons and presentations and make them even stronger! You'll discover simple adjustments, tips, and techniques to help learners understand and absorb Bible points and to bring your learning environment to life.

And with that, let's jump back to other (non-Group) training resources that I've found incredibly useful.

- *How to Win Friends & Influence People* by Dale Carnegie (Simon & Schuster). Yes, this is a secular book, so you might need to eat the meat and spit out the bones here. But it's still a classic, and in my opinion, no book has said it better. There's a reason it's been in print since 1937 and has sold more than 15 million copies.
- *Made to Stick: Why Some Ideas Survive and Others Die,* by Chip and Dan Heath (Random House). OK, maybe I take the above claim back—*this* one might be the best. It's all about how to make your ideas stick to others' brains. Tons of great stories! It's fascinating how Jesus employed all six of their principles—it's as if he knew! (And he did.)

If you're not comfortable with secular resources, check out similar books by Christian authors.

- *The 21 Irrefutable Laws of Leadership: Follow Them and People Will Follow You,* by John C. Maxwell (Thomas Nelson). This is a leadership classic and sure to help you develop your group's people skills, leadership skills, and team-building skills. I love this book.
- *The Seven Laws of the Learner,* by Bruce Wilkinson (Multnomah). The best book on teaching I've read. The video series that accompanies it is especially helpful. I've been through it a couple of times and need to do so again.
- *Just Walk Across the Room: Simple Steps Pointing People to Faith,* by Bill Hybels (Zondervan). This book, and his earlier work, *Becoming a Contagious Christian* (with Mark Mittelberg, also Zondervan) are two classics in the field of faith sharing.

There are more good resources to train teachers today than there have ever been. These are busy days. But people need training, and effective churches will find a way to get it done.

There's one more thing that group leaders desperately need from their pastor-leaders.

Rewarding

Extensive research has demonstrated the value of rewarding people. Adrian Gostick and Chester Elton, authors of *The Carrot Principle,* worked with Healthstream Research to quantify a huge amount of data, including more than 200,000 interviews with managers and employees around the world. Here are a few of their findings:

- In response to the question, "My organization recognizes excellence," the organizations that scored in the bottom 25 percent had an average return on equity (ROE) of 2.4 percent, whereas those scoring in the top 25 percent had an average ROE of 8.7 percent.
- Teams and offices rated most highly by employees as doing a good job of recognizing employee contributions also typically placed in the top scores for customer satisfaction, employee satisfaction, and retention.
- Of those who report the highest morale at work, 94.4 percent said their managers are effective at recognition. In contrast, 56 percent of employees who reported low morale gave managers a failing grade on recognition.[7]

These findings apply to leadership within the church, too. Recognize your people. Reward them. Here are some ideas to help you get started:

An appreciation dinner where *everyone's* appreciated. I shared a great example of this idea in Chapter 4. The important thing is that you come up with a way to recognize and reward everyone during the course of the evening, and that you do it in a way that also recognizes each person's unique contributions.

Gifts, of all sizes and at all times. Gifts almost always work as rewards. I've seen a number of hosts pass out prizes at conferences. Occasionally they're given as rewards for specific accomplishments by individual teachers, but more often they're random door prizes. Participants put their names in the hat, and those whose names are drawn get items like gift cards and popular books.

Richard King, minister of educationin Las Cruces, New Mexico, is fond of passing out Dairy Queen gift cards. They're fairly inexpensive, and he passes out lots of them. Again, no matter how you do it, everyone should get rewarded somehow. We need to say thank you to everyone for the work they do.

Bring them up front. Bring groups up on the stage or in front of the congregation to recognize and reward them. *Everyone* in the group. Not just leaders—*everyone. Everyone* contributes to the growth of a group. Acknowledge that contribution, and reinforce the idea so *everyone* understands that.

Feeding frenzy! Some churches do even more. I know churches that have bought dinners for the fastest-growing groups in their church. The whole class, not just the teacher, gets a dinner. Again, it's another opportunity to acknowledge that every member of the group is important.

Praise board. I've gotten more ideas about how to reward people via Facebook. Here's one from Shelly Nichols: Create a "praise board." Anyone can use sticky notes to make positive comments about others. They can sign the note or leave it anonymous. Post it where everyone has access. All the praise doesn't have to come from you to be powerful and meaningful, you know.

Spouses are a gift—so give *them* a gift, too. Here's another Facebook idea, from fundraising consultant Kris Wood: Hand out gifts to the spouses of those serving. Thank them for giving up so much time with their spouses so they can serve the church.

Award plaques. I used to give recognition through a series of plaques. There were four per year, one for each age division—preschool, children, youth, and adults. Each plaque had 12 small plates, one for each month of the year. Each month, I'd put the name of the fastest-growing class in that age division for that month. By doing it this way, there were many more winners because "fastest-growing" was determined by comparing each group against itself. If a group did really well one month, its success made it more difficult to win the following month—and therefore gave other groups a better opportunity to win.

Resources are rewards, too. Buy your leaders commentaries, Bible dictionaries, and popular trade books. This is a reward that does double duty. The resources let the teacher know that you appreciate his or her effort, but they also help that leader become an even better leader.

Bankroll your groups' parties. When David Francis, head of Sunday school for Lifeway Christian Resources, was a minister of education, he gave group leaders cold hard cash they could use toward parties. (Well, it was actually money in an account that they would later use for parties, but it translated into cash.) This reward also did a double duty—it encouraged groups to increase attendance and at the same time, made it easier for the groups to have more parties.

Reward completed training. Give a gift card to everyone who completes a certain training course. If a teacher or leader invested a significant amount of personal time in reading books or taking an online course for more training, this reward might be especially valuable. That teacher spent a lot of time working to be a better teacher. Find a way to say thank you.

Budget for rewards. Rewards cost money. And most churches can't do what they don't budget for. So put it in the budget. Set aside money to reward behavior, and set aside other funds to reward results.

***Always* say thank you.** If a group has a party and invites every member and every prospect, acknowledge and thank the people who organized it, even if they didn't get any newcomers. If newcomers didn't attend, they'll *need* encouragement. When the party goes really well, the success of the party is its own reward. When no one shows up, tell your leaders, "Thank you for putting in the effort; hang in there, the fruit will come."

All this talk of reward might strike you as a bit secular or worldly, but really it's not. God is a rewarder. We should follow God's example whenever we can.

So let's recap. If you're a pastor, there are four major areas in which you can help your groups grow:

- Lead by example. Model what you want to see done.
- Become your groups' biggest cheerleader. Promote your groups. Encourage them.
- Provide training that equips teachers with the skills we've discussed throughout this book.

• Reward your groups—*everyone* in your groups. Remember: Whatever gets rewarded gets done.

Use any of the ideas I've provided here—or better yet, use them as inspiration to come up with your own ideas. We serve the ultimate Creator, so ask God what these ideas might look like in *your* church.

Now we turn to some final thoughts and applications for leaders.

leaders, go forth: a 10-step strategy

We've come a long way together. And we have a long way to go. So I'd like to summarize the findings of this book by offering a 10-step strategy for implementing those findings and provide some practical ideas for what that might look like in your church. Again, don't feel restricted to using only the ideas in my list. Every church is different. The Spirit works differently in every church. Find your own way, and allow this final chapter to prod you to seek what God wants to do in *your* church and with *your* groups.

Which brings us nicely to our first step.

1. Pray.

The Bible teaches that apart from Jesus we can do nothing (see John 15:5). It doesn't say that we'll be slightly more effective as we remain in Christ; it says that without abiding in Christ, we can't accomplish *anything* of lasting spiritual significance. The data from my surveys underlines the fact that spiritual vibrancy and numerical growth normally go hand-in-hand and that, likewise, there's also a strong correlation between faith and numerical growth. This is a healthy reminder that we need to begin with prayer, end with prayer, and pray at all points between. To paraphrase the words of E.M. Bounds: The church is looking for better methods; God is looking for better people, people of prayer.

I preached a message on Philippians 1:3 not too long ago: "Every time I think of you, I give thanks to my God." One of the inescapable things about teaching is that it's difficult to not listen to your own message. I might be able to put others to sleep, but I can't sleep through my own message!

As I meditated on how I could apply this message to my own life, I came up with an idea. I brought my camera to church and took pictures of all the people at my church, in groups of two to four, and then had a collage of those pictures printed on a coffee mug—which I drink from as I pray and read my Bible in the morning. As I drink from that mug and look at that picture, I give thanks to God for the people in my church and my group.

Here are some more ways to give thanks for *your* group and get them engaged in prayer from the get-go:

Get them started. Don't assume that people will be comfortable praying out loud, especially if it's their first time in a group. Don't call on someone to pray out loud unless you know ahead of time that he or she is comfortable doing so or have asked beforehand. If it's a first meeting in which people don't know each other well, ask for prayer requests. Simply ask, "How can we as a group pray for you this week?" Then lead a closing prayer for your group.

Break it down. Form pairs or smaller groups for prayer. People are more likely to share personal requests in a more intimate setting.

"Popcorn" prayers. Ask people to take turns completing a simple one-sentence prayer. For example, "Lord, I want to thank you for…" or "Lord, help me to become closer to you in…"

Be still and know… Don't overlook the power of silent prayer. Your group members may feel comfortable telling each other what they need prayer for and still feel more comfortable praying silently. The fact that *you're* not hearing it doesn't mean *God's* not listening.

Pray Scripture together. The Lord's Prayer is a good example, as are the Psalms. You can pray together or break up the passage into parts. This may also make it easier for your "non-pray-ers" to pray aloud.

Conversational prayer. This is one of my favorite ways to pray as a group. As if they were in a conversation, people pray in random order, as long or as briefly as they want, and they can choose to participate or just listen.

Prayer chain. A prayer chain is an old-fashioned but effective way of passing along prayer needs in a group. Just because the idea has been around for a while doesn't mean it doesn't still work. Some groups have people pray together over the phone as they pass prayer needs along.

An e-mailed prayer list is a common practice for many groups these days. My mom does this for her group. She writes down the prayer requests during group time and types them up when she gets home. By e-mailing them to everyone in the group, those who weren't able to attend can stay connected to the group and stay in prayer for needs that were shared.

The single most important thing a leader can do for his or her group is to spend time in prayer for group members. So what are you waiting for? Take a minute and pray for your group right now.

Done? Good. Now let's have some fun—literally.

2. Have a party.

People often ask me, "What kind of party should I have?"

My answer: "Whatever sounds *fun* to you!"

People have even asked me, "How do you apply this idea for youth?" My answer: "What other way is there to *do* youth ministry? Isn't this how youth ministry is normally done?" This is really more about adapting youth-ministry principles to adult ministry than the other way around.

Others will say, "I teach senior adults. They don't like to get out after dark. What kind of parties would you recommend for us?" I encourage them (and you) to try something before dark, perhaps a lunch meeting.

There are as many different possibilities as there are different people.

Here are some tried-and-true ideas to get you started. Use all of them, or create your own parties for your own people.

Calendar events. You'll discover at least half a dozen good party ideas, just by looking through the calendar—including New Year's Eve, Memorial Day, Fourth of July, Labor Day, and Christmas. Try a swimming party for a summer get-together, and plan a Fall Family Festival on Halloween. Organize a Super Bowl party, and if Groundhog Day's your thing, rent the movie and celebrate that, too.

Short and long. We normally think of parties as weekend, 7-to-10 kind of events. Those will certainly work, but also consider holding events at other times or events that run longer than one evening. Shorter events include a meal after church, breakfast before church, or lunch during the week. For longer events, think about things like softball season, if your church has a softball team, and make time to gather after each game. Consider a weekend retreat. I know groups that have done a full-week vacation together. (That's actually more community than even *I* require!)

Expensive and cheap. Our group has done ski days, which aren't cheap. On the whole, however, we try to do things that are less expensive. Nearly anyone can afford a potluck dinner. Game night is one of our favorite things to do, and it's almost free.

Guy things/gal things. Try both as they fit the makeup of your group. We have a tea room here in Las Cruces that provides frilly hats for the ladies to wear while they're eating. Not a lot of guys eat at the tea room. David Murrow, in his book *Why Men Hate Going to Church,* astutely pointed out that many churches tend to favor the feminine side and that they'd do well to lean into doing more masculine things as well.[1] At the end of the day, we want some of both.

General interest/specific interest. We tend to stay away from things like golf or skiing or bridge because we figure not everyone skis or plays golf or bridge. However, it's not a bad idea to occasionally do things that *are* very specific in their appeal. If you do a golf scramble, not everyone will be interested, but the ones who are interested will be *really* interested.

Spontaneous/planned events. Most events will be planned so that you can maximize involvement. People will come if we give them ample notice. However, there's something to be said for spur-of-the-moment events. We recently had a hamburger cookout at our home. I started making phone calls about noon on Saturday, and by two we had a rough idea of how many would come. By six, burgers were coming off the grill.

Fun things/service things. For some, service is more fun than the usual "fun" things. This is true of people outside the church as well as inside. Do a movie night for fun; do a "move *me*" night as a service project. Do a game night for fun; volunteer to paint a school for a service project.

The key here is variety. Do as many different kinds of service as you can think of. The more variety you have, the more likely you are to engage everyone.

3. Evaluate and adjust.

So, did everyone have a good time?

If you and your group aren't having fun, you won't sustain momentum, and this plan won't work. If you haven't hit the right chord this first time around, find something that *is* genuinely fun for people in your group. Even if turnout wasn't what you hoped for, you and your group need to get satisfaction from a feeling that you would have done the activity anyway.

Our group often enjoys a dinner-and-a-movie night. One time, no one showed up. If you do this kind of thing enough, it's going to happen to you, too. Count on it. So what did my wife and I do when no one showed up? We watched the movie. We were going to do it anyway.

As I speak to groups about this, many group members tense up and respond with something like, "What could I do that would be interesting to someone else?" I'd encourage you to think about it from the opposite angle: What do you *like* doing, and how could you build *that* into an outreach opportunity?

I emphasize the point that it's crucial that people in the group enjoy being together. It has to work for the group before it will work for outsiders. If people in the group aren't enjoying being together, outsiders aren't going to imagine themselves joining them. If the group doesn't enjoy being together, it won't endure.

People often complain that they're too busy to work this plan. But the fact is, people are almost *never* too busy to do what they *really* enjoy doing.

It may sound a little selfish, but the focus of your first round of evaluation should be this: Did people in my group enjoy being together, and did I enjoy being with them? Is this something we'd gladly do every month, even if no one else comes? If the answer is yes, you're ready to proceed to the next step.

If not, take a step back and figure out what you *would* enjoy doing. Ask, Why didn't we enjoy being together? What was boring or unpleasant? What do we need to do that's different? Answering this last question is your easiest solution—as long as you *can* find something different to enjoy.

Here are a few other suggestions, to help you process through this stage:

Try lots of stuff. You'll never know what you like until you try. A game night might not sound like all that much fun to some, but you never know. Once you get past the learning curve, it might really catch on. To quote a line from an old commercial, "Try it—you'll like it!"

Consider the makeup of your group. Generally speaking, the more people have in common, the easier it is for a group to gel. This works well up to a point. I have seen larger churches thinly slice classes by age to the point where it's just silly. It makes more sense to organize groups around affinity of some kind.

New Life Church in Colorado Springs organizes groups entirely around common interests—groups for people who like to hike, groups for people who like to ride mountain bikes, groups for people who home-school their kids, and groups for people who like to ski. This may seem an extreme or perhaps frivolous approach to some, but the underlying principle of organizing around affinity is a good one. The more people have in common, the more likely they'll enjoy being together.

Put them on probation. Some churches follow a semester-by-semester approach, rather than a permanent grouping. Using this approach, people can "date" a group before they commit to it. If the group really gels, people can choose to stay together permanently.

Time is on your side. The more time we spend together, the more we relax and enjoy being together. People tend to grow on us in time. If you haven't been in the habit of getting together, whatever you do is not going to be all that much fun at first. Once the group really gels and enjoys being together, *what* you do doesn't matter as much.

4. *Now,* invite guests.

Up to this point, I haven't said anything about inviting anyone but friends. There was a reason for that. You need to have a positive group of friends first. Until you have a group of friends who genuinely love each other and enjoy being together, you don't have anything to invite people to. At least not anything they'll want to stick around for.

But now that you've established a groundwork of meaningful and enjoyable relationships, it's time to invite other people. A good place to start is with absentees and recent visitors to your church—particularly if the absentees from your church haven't been absent *too* long. The longer people have been absent, the more difficult it is to get them back. The Bible teaches that we're to care for everyone, not just people with good church attendance.

One of the best and most natural ways to get absentees back is to invite them to parties regularly.

People who visit your church are some of the easiest-to-reach people. There's something to be said for going after these "low-hanging fruit." Invite them to your parties, and see what happens.

Earlier we talked about the various kinds of parties you can have. Use variety, too, in the ways you invite folks. I talked to someone once who was struggling to make the party plan work. I leaned in for some details.

"How did you go about promoting the parties?"

"We announced it three times in class."

It seemed like an insight from the land of *duh!* that the people they hoped would come weren't in class and therefore weren't hearing these announcements.

Use every available means to let people know about the party.

Phone calls. This remains my personal favorite method of contact. And don't try to be too efficient, getting in as many calls in as little time as possible. Take a minute to ask how life is going, and wait for people to respond. Group life is all about relationships, and you don't have to wait for the party for that to happen. As a general rule, it's best that guys call guys and gals call gals—especially in singles' groups. This way there's no misunderstanding the intent of the caller.

Mail: Old-fashioned, but still effective. When was the last time you saw a hand-addressed envelope in your mailbox? When was the last time you didn't read it? (I'm guessing never.) Send a written invitation to every member and every potential member every month. If cost is a problem, your church might be able to help with the expense of stamps and supplies, or pool your resources as a group.

E-mail. E-mail is so quick and easy and free that it makes sense to send multiple e-mails—one a week or two before the event and one a day or two before the event. Don't be obnoxious with the frequency of your e-mails, but do use them enough to be effective.

They're called social networks for a reason. As I write this, Facebook, Twitter, and texting are emerging as the new technologies for groups to latch on to. By the time you read this, there may be totally new technologies to help us. While I encourage you to embrace these, remember this: Sometimes the inefficient, old-fashioned technology is meaningful because it *does* take more effort. People know that it takes more care to hand-address an envelope than to send a mass e-mail or tweet.

Oh, and don't forget to announce it during group time!

5. Evaluate and adjust again.

Perhaps you're starting to see a pattern here. Too much ministry is "ministry by pronouncement." That is, we decide what to do, announce it to the group, and implement it, expecting immediate success as we do.

A better approach is to dabble and experiment. Try lots of stuff. See what works. Keep that and discard the rest. Jim Collins and Jerry Porras talk about this in their bestseller *Built to Last,* a study of some of the most successful companies over the past 100 years. The title of Chapter 7 is "Try a Lot of Stuff and Keep What Works."[2] Now's the time for you to do that, too.

Ask, Did anyone come? Do we need to do something different that would be more interesting to other kinds of people? Experiment with all kinds of parties. Once people respond, be more aggressive about inviting other people who aren't familiar with your church, such as people you know from work or from your neighborhood.

I talked with one man one who was good at inviting people. First he'd invite people to various events that would appeal to them. Then he'd invite them to church where, to their surprise, they'd discover that they already knew a bunch of the people. They'd feel totally at home and welcomed.

Here are some more ideas for evaluating your progress:

How'd they like it? Your first round of evaluating and adjusting centered on the question, Did we like it? This time, the key question is, Did *the people we invited* like it? Was it fun for them as well as us?

Evaluation can be done in several ways. A simple conversation with you and the leaders in the group may be enough. From time to time, take some time as a group to evaluate how you're doing. Is what you're doing getting the results you want?

Vision Day. This one is explained in more detail in Chapter 4. Every quarter—or at least once a year—devote an entire session to evaluating how you're doing. You might discuss all the parties you did through the year and how people felt about each one. I'd also suggest bringing a list of members and potential members for people to look at. As often as people review the list, someone is sure to say, "Hey, the Johnsons. I forgot about them. We need to give them a call." This is the purpose of evaluation: to improve what we do.

The power of anonymity. Sometimes your best information will come as you give people the opportunity to provide feedback privately. Online surveys are quick and easy and often free. They allow you to quantify your results. It's one thing to say, "Everyone seemed to have fun." It's quite another to say, "Ninety-one percent of the people who came to the retreat said they'd come again if we did it next year."

Again, it may take a while to perfect this plan in your particular context. This is not meant to be a checklist. Coming up with a plan that works for your group requires dabbling and experimenting, evaluating and adjusting. Give yourself permission to fail. And more importantly, give your group permission to do even better.

6. Start developing a team.

By now you should be seeing progress. Some of the insiders are starting to get it. So get them more involved. It's fun, but it also takes work. Here are some ideas to start developing a team.

Give people permission to test-drive. Don't ask people to make a one-year commitment. Ask them to help with a party or make phone calls. Let people stick their toes in the water before they dive in.

Look for God-given talent. Strengths tend to show up pretty early. If someone is good at something, you'll probably know it right away. Think about the early rounds of *American Idol*. Sometimes you know from the auditions who'll make the top 10.

I remember hearing one guy teach for the first time. I couldn't believe it. He seemed better than 90 percent of the teachers I had, and this was his first day. We can coach skill, but only God can give talent and spiritual gifting. Look for it.

Look for passion. We do our best work in the area of our passion. Some are passionate about missions, some music, some teaching, some kids. As much as possible, allow people to move toward the area of their passion.

Cultivate an atmosphere of grace. Allow people to try things and fail. Allow them to experiment. Allow them to get better. If people are criticized every time they try and don't get it right, you'll soon have a very small team.

Share the wealth. One group I was a part of had an annual planning meeting in December. At this meeting, the group would plan the calendar for the entire year. Seasonal events would go on the calendar first, followed by the rest of the fellowships, until we had about one event a month. Then we'd take turns volunteering to be on teams to plan the parties. This way, we spread the work around.

Don't try to do it all yourself. Get lots of people involved.

7. Pump up the people skills.

Do an honest evaluation of your people skills. Can you get along well with difficult people and people who are different from you? Read a book or two. Ask a friend how you could do better. Role-play so you both can polish your skills.

One of my follow-up surveys related directly to the issue of people skills. There were three interesting findings that came out of that survey. Take advantage of them all.

Cell-phone use. I asked leaders how many members' phone numbers they had programmed into their cell phones. My suspicion was this: Leaders of growing groups would likely have more numbers programmed because they contacted their group members on a more regular basis. Turns out my suspicion was right. Rapidly growing classes were more than twice as likely (112 percent) to have 10 or more class members' phone numbers programmed into their cells.

So make it easy for yourself. Get your group members' numbers in your cell. Then call them and say, "Let's go get a pizza!"

Where are your best friends? I asked how many people in their group would say, "My best friends attend my group." Again, rapidly growing groups were more than twice as likely (105 percent) to have five or more people who said their best friends attended group, too. What do we learn from this? Rapidly growing classes, normally, are groups of tightly knit friends. This also puts to rest the myth that non-growing groups are relationally closer. People sometimes fear outreach because they think it will disrupt existing friendships. The opposite is true—relationships help groups grow.

I like this group! I also asked, "To what degree do you agree (or disagree) with this statement: 'I *really* like my group'?" The results were even more pronounced—rapidly growing groups were *more than three and a half times* more likely to strongly agree. People often say to me, "I don't know if we want to grow our group. We're just happy the way we are." The research suggests that they'd be even happier if they embraced the vision of growing their groups—and their circles of friends.

What emerges from these findings is a picture of group life that's very different from what I find in some churches. Again, this group life is not so much an organized program that's part of a strategy reach a goal. Rather, it's a tightly knit group of friends who enjoy doing life together. If you don't have good people skills, the joy in being together never materializes. Here are some ideas on how to use your social skills to help cultivate that joy.

Watch your tone. The Bible says "a gentle answer," not a short answer. The tone of your voice has as much to do with your success with people as just about anything else.

Quick to listen, slow to speak. Remember the one-second pause. Make sure people have finished talking before you respond. Reflect their words back to them, making sure you understood them correctly. It feels so good to be heard!

Proactive kindness. One of my favorite Old Testament stories is in 2 Samuel 9, where David asked, "Is anyone in Saul's family still alive—anyone to whom I can show kindness for Jonathan's sake?" (2 Samuel 9:1). David didn't have to be kind. No request came clamoring to his desk. He just sat down one day and thought, "How could I do something kind?" The rest of the story? David's people found Mephibosheth, who was crippled in both feet, "And from that time on, Mephibosheth ate regularly at David's table, like one of the king's own sons" (2 Samuel 9:11b).

We ought to do the same. From time to time, we should put our feet up and think, "Who can I be nice to today—for no reason other than I just *feel* like it?"

Bear with one another. There are really only two ways a relationship can go bad—I can offend you, or you can offend me. Most of my suggestions on good people skills focus on the former. The latter is equally important—don't be easily offended. The Bible says, "Bear with each other and forgive whatever grievances you may have against one another. Forgive as the Lord forgave you" (Colossians 3:13, NIV). Bearing with others assumes there's something to bear with. It assumes you will irritate me. There is a place to confront and a place to let it go. Easily offended people are seldom used greatly by God.

Guard your heart. Keep your own self together so you can serve others. It is hard to display good people skills when you're in a bad mood. Keep your cup full so that you can pour into others. Grumpy people are seldom used greatly by God. People whose hearts are full of the love of God are rarely offended by others.

Don't brush over this topic too quickly. Again, people almost universally rate themselves higher in people skills than they really are. All of us can do better. All of us would do well to make a lifelong commitment to improving our people skills.

8. Increase your spiritual vibrancy.

Above all else, guard your heart. Spend time in the Word. Spend time in worship. Keep the fire of your devotion hot. Do as many of these as you can, and add more of your own:

Read. My life has been greatly enriched by reading books. Yours can be, too. Read books that inspire you to live for God. John Piper, C.S. Lewis, R.C. Sproul, and Henry Blackaby are just a few of my personal favorites. You'll have your own. Find them. Spend time with them as you would your friends in your group. Discover how God has worked in their lives. Learn from their triumphs—and struggles. Discover what God might be trying to tell you through other stories and discoveries.

Listen to music. Find music that inspires you to worship and draws you closer to God. Countless times, while I was driving long distances between conferences, God has turned my car into a sanctuary. There's just something about music that opens our hearts to God.

Listen to sermons. Discover those pastors and speakers who warm your heart and renew your mind. With the advent of podcasts, it's easier and more convenient than ever to listen to the greatest living speakers, as well as some twentieth-century speakers who are no longer living but whose words are still alive.

Spend time in the Word and in prayer. The fundamental discipline of the Christian life is spending time with God. God speaks to us through his Word; we speak to God through prayer (and God speaks back).

Worship together. It's never been easier to worship as a group, even if you don't have musicians in your group. DVD-based worship resources are as close as your nearest Christian or online bookstore. With a big-screen TV and a good sound system, you can turn a living room into a worshipful concert experience for your small group.

Retreat! There's nothing like getting away from it all with your group for a few days to partake in spiritually stimulating nourishment. With the help of a TV screen and DVD player, you can bring some of the top speakers with you wherever you go. Or you could give each other the opportunity to lead a session, and allow people in your group to develop their God-given skills in a safe environment. One of the nice things about a retreat setting is that you can watch and discuss. The routine of life often limits our time. Take an extended time together when you can to worship, listen to God's Word, and find fellowship together.

Become a student of yourself. Gary Thomas, in his excellent book *Sacred Pathways,* illustrates that different people connect with God in different ways.[3] Some connect with God in big groups; others require solitude. Some like loud, rowdy music, while others prefer a more serene atmosphere. Be a student of yourself. Find out what best connects you with God—and then, get connected!

Talk to the people in your group about these things often. Ask how they're doing with their time alone (or collectively, if that's how they're built) with God. Most people need regular accountability to keep them doing what they really do intend to do.

9. Cultivate your group's faith.

Most groups that have grown first believed they *could* grow. They expected to grow. They expected God to bless. They expected God to move. They expected greater things to happen. We, too, will see it when we believe it. Try the following suggestions to help build up your group's faith and confidence.

Celebrate small wins. I started pastoring a small church recently. The first month I was there, we had 18 people in three groups. Six months later, we had 24 people. My wife also just started a new group. From one perspective, a growth of six people in six months is a pretty small win. From another perspective, that number reflects 33 percent growth. If we maintain that pace, we can expect a great harvest as the years go by. Celebrate small wins.

Keep score, but keep your eye on the ball. Imagine a group of guys casually shooting hoops. The atmosphere is relaxed until someone says, "Let's get into teams and keep score." Suddenly the atmosphere is charged with energetic competition. Elbows fly. So does sweat. Shoes squeak on the hard wood. Keeping score motivates us to do our best.

At the same time, don't make too much of numbers. Coach John Wooden was famous for teaching each player to play his best and let the score take care of itself. Develop a system of keeping score without getting obsessed with numbers.

By pointing out to your group that you've grown, you instill in the group the belief that you can continue to grow in the future.

Rub shoulders with leaders whose groups are growing. Faith is contagious. As you spend time with leaders who are growing their groups, their confident expectation will rub off on you.

You might contact other churches in town and ask them which small-group leaders in their church are really getting it done. Take those small group leaders out to lunch and talk to them about their ministries. And don't go alone. The goal is to strengthen not only *your* faith but the faith of your group.

You'll find more success stories like these at makeyourgroupgrow.com (see the end of Chapter 7). We dream of an online community where you'll be able to swap stories with teachers who are growing and ask questions to clarify the way. Doing so will strengthen your faith, as well as the faith of the people in your group.

10. Pray. (Yes, again.)

Begin with prayer, and end with prayer. And pray at all points between. Without Christ we can do nothing. We can do all things through Christ. And as you continue working through these steps again, pray more and more.

One final question

Why? Why would we want to grow a group, anyway?

You came to this book with your own reasons for answering that question. I'd like to add a dozen of my own. Some of these reasons might look a lot like yours, some may not. But consider them all, and if some aren't on your list, add them.

Reason 1: It's fun! Growing a group is more fun than Six Flags. People in growing churches and growing groups are having more fun. They laugh more. They hug more. They smile more. Our research touched on this aspect a number of times and demonstrated what I already knew: Growing groups have more fun—and more joy.

Reason 2: People need to know Jesus. It's exciting to grow a group, but it's not all fun and games. This is serious business. The eternal soul of every person who attends is on the line. We have an enemy who shoots with real bullets, and this is not a dress rehearsal. There are no do-overs. So let's take our fun seriously.

Reason 3: We have the cure. Politicians and pundits constantly debate which party has the best solutions to our nation's problems. Here's my take: None of them do. The solution is not a political solution. Politics does not have the answer. Psychology, sociology, education, or more money is not the answer. Jesus is the answer. And we need new hearts to receive that answer—hearts that know God's love and grace and forgiveness and are willing and able to give that love and grace and forgiveness to others. Helping groups to grow is one of the best methods I know of to spread that message.

Reason 4: All the lonely people. Ever been lonely? Ever been *really* lonely? I have, and I can tell you, it stinks.

Occasionally you'll hear someone say, "Christianity is all about a loving relationship with God." I don't think that's quite right. It is not *all* about a loving relationship with God. It is also about a loving relationship with people. God's people. And that includes those who don't yet *know* they're God's people. We need each other. We need a loving community of Christians who'll represent God to us in a thousand day-to-day ways.

Reason 5: We *can* do it! The most common pair of prayers I've prayed over my entire life go like this: "Father, I confess my awareness that without you I can do nothing," and "I confess my strong confidence that we can do all things through Christ who strengthens us."

We really *can* grow a group. We really *can* create new groups. We really *can* make a difference in a hurting, sick world, one life at a time.

Reason 6: Groups *are* the church. The church exists on several levels. First of all, there's the universal, invisible church. We also normally think of our local church. But, in a profound sense, the small group is a microcosm of the church. The book of Acts speaks of both big meetings in the temple courts and small meetings in homes.

There's some debate these days about the comparative merits of home groups versus on-campus groups. That is, to me, an adventure in missing the point. Wherever your group meets, *that* is the church. God's plan for reaching the world was through the growth of the church. As these micro-churches grow, the church will inevitably grow.

Reason 7: The power of multiplication. Think of a group that grows from 10 to 14 members in nine months. At that same rate of growth (40 percent every nine months) this same group would reach 1,000 people in 10 years and the world in 43. It may not look like much at first, but if you can perfect the skill of growing groups, you won't be able to build buildings fast enough to contain the growth. There is no better plan under heaven than to give the ministry to everyday Christians who can use their God-given gifts to grow their groups.

Reason 8: Joy, joy, joy. Earlier I spoke of the joy of the work. Here I am thinking of the joy that's ours in Jesus. I love living the Christian life—don't you? I really *do* get up many mornings—hopefully most mornings—and say, "I love living the Christian life!"

I love knowing God walks with me and talks with me and tells me I am his own. I love knowing I'm forgiven of all of my sins. I love it that when I think of death, the first thought that comes to mind is "better by far" (Philippians 1:23). I love the work. I love having a reason to get out of bed in the morning. I love knowing God has given me something to do—something *God* wants *me* to do.

For all these reasons and so many more, I love living the Christian life. And I want others to know the joy that is ours in Jesus. I want my group to grow so that others can know the joy that I know.

Reason 9: Jesus *told* us to grow. Somewhere along the line, we come to the point of spiritual maturity where I realize that God is God and I am not. God is boss; I am not. God is master; I am his slave. God speaks; I do as he says. Jesus told us to go and make disciples of all nations. Jesus told us that following him would make us fishers of men. The Master has spoken, and he has not stuttered. We are to obey. And there is unspeakable joy in that, too.

Reason 10: The reward is great. The Bible teaches we are saved by grace through faith. Rewards, however, are given on the basis of works. Consider these verses:

- "For the Son of Man is going to come in his Father's glory with his angels, and then he will reward each person according to what he has done" (Matthew 16:27).
- "Look, I am coming soon, bringing my reward with me to repay all people according to their deeds" (Revelation 22:12).

Those who work hard will be greatly rewarded.

Reason 11: Because of all Jesus has done for *us*. I love the way The Living Bible communicates Romans 12:1. Here's how it presents the last line of the verse: "When you think of what he has done for you, is this too much to ask?"

It really *isn't* too much to ask. Anyone who has watched the movie *The Passion of the Christ* knows it's not too much to ask. Anyone who fully—or even partially—understands what Jesus has done for us knows it's not too much to ask.

In 2 Corinthians 5:14, Paul wrote, "Christ's love compels us." The context suggests that it is Christ's love as demonstrated on the cross that compels us. The Greek word translated as *compel* suggests that we have no other choice. When we think of what Jesus did for us on the cross, we are compelled to lay down our lives for the cause of Jesus.

The old hymn by Isaac Watts says it best:

When I survey the wondrous cross,
On which the Prince of glory died,
My richest gain I count but loss,
And pour contempt on all my pride.

Were the whole realm of nature mine,
That were a present far too small;
Love so amazing, so divine,
Demands my soul, my life, my all.

The cross demands my soul, my life, my all. There are a million ways you could express that truth. Explore as many of them as you can in this life. One good way is by dedicating ourselves to microcosms of the church—small groups that are committed to growing.

Reason 12: For the glory of God. When you fall in love with Jesus, you want him to be treated better than he is treated. You want him to be respected and loved and honored and enjoyed. Growing groups are a great way to get more people to treat him better . The glory of God compels us. It is all about the glory of God.

May God bless each one of you as he helps your group—his group, his *church*—grow!

o   MAKE YOUR GROUP GROW

the surveys

Survey #1

This first survey served as the core of this book. Respondents were not a scientifically random sample; rather, they were, for the most part, people who attend my seminars and visit my web page. Several other surveys were conducted. See makemygroupgrow.com for details.

1. Would you describe your class as

Declining 10%

Stable 48%

Growing 39%

Growing rapidly 4%

2. How would you rate your strength in the following areas?

TEACHING ABILITY

1 star 1.6%

2 stars 5.8%

3 stars 32.5%

4 stars 46.6%

5 stars 13.4%

PEOPLE SKILLS

1 star 0.9%

2 stars 5.4%

3 stars 27.0%

4 stars 45.5%

5 stars 21.2%

SPIRITUAL VIBRANCY

1 star 1.4%

2 stars 4.9%

3 stars 35.4%

4 stars 43.6%

5 stars 14.6%

ORGANIZATIONAL SKILL

1 star 3.7%

2 stars 15.3%

3 stars 32.1%

4 stars 29.6%

5 stars 19.3%

3. Do you participate in visitation?

Rarely / never 29%

Occasionally / sporadically . .46%

Regularly / consistently 25%

4. How many fellowships do you have a year?

0–4 . . . . 47%

5–8 . . . . 30%

9 or more 23%

5. Of the time you spend in ministry, what percentage would you say is spent on

preparation for the lesson 55%

ministry and relationship

building 45%

6. What percentage of your time do you spend ministering to people

inside the class 61%

outside of the class. . 39%

7. Where do you expect your class to be a year from now?

Stable 21%

Growing 68%

Growing rapidly 11%

8. How many class officers (i.e., in-reach leaders, outreach leaders, fellowship leaders, etc.) do you have for your class?

None (only me) 25%

One 13%

Two 19%

Three 12%

More than three 30%

9. Would you say the purpose of your class (communicated as a percentage) is mostly about growing the class spiritually or reaching out to outsiders?

Growing the members

spiritually 69%

Reaching out to outsiders. . . .31%

10. How does your group feel about the idea of growing and dividing your group?

Openly embraces the vision of

growing and dividing 33%

Ambivalent about growing

and dividing 36%

Mildly opposed to the vision

of growing and dividing 19%

Strongly opposed to the idea

of dividing our group 12%

Survey #2

The first survey made me curious about a few things, so I conducted a second survey. Of the questions on that survey, the following were used in this book:

How many people has your group sent out to work in other areas (preschool, children, etc.) in the past year?

None 26%

One 10%

Two or three 32%

Four or five 14%

More than six 18%

How many have come to faith in Christ through your group in the past 12 months?

None 56%

One 18%

Two or three. 18%

Four or more 7%

Do you have an officially designated teacher-in-training?

Yes 32%

No 68%

Do you have specific, clearly defined goals for your group?

Yes 43%

No 57%

Survey #3
Spiritual vibrancy

I used this survey to drill deeper into what created an atmosphere of spiritual vibrancy. The questions or statements in quotes below were asked this way verbatim; people seemed to grasp the ideas well enough.

"The atmosphere in my class is positive and uplifting."

Strongly agree 46%

Agree. 46%

Neutral 7%

Disagree 1%

Strongly disagree. 0%

Would you describe the teaching in this group as

very practical in its application

of truths to life. 60%

somewhat practical in its

application of truths to life . . . 28%

mostly content delivery with

some application 11%

almost all content delivery

with little application. 2%

"It is *always* in *my* best interest to obey God."

Strongly agree 89%

Agree. 10%

Neutral 1%

Disagree 1%

Strongly disagree. 0%

"I feel loved by the people in my group."

Strongly agree 43%

Agree. 49%

Neutral 7%

Disagree 1%

Strongly disagree 1%

Survey #4:
Fall 2009 Survey

The more questions I asked, the more questions I raised. In this case, I was curious about how specific behaviors, such as cell-phone use and how people in the group felt about the group, affected the growth of a group. The picture that emerged and was brought into even sharper focus was this: A growing group is usually a tightly knit group of friends who really like each other and enjoy being together.

Approximately how many of your group members' phone numbers do you have in your cell phone?

1	12%
2	.8%
3	.6%
4	10%
5	.9%
6	.7%
7	.2%
8	.5%
9	.1%
10 or more	39%

How many people in your group would say, "My best friends attend my group"?

0	.8%
1	.8%
2	26%
3	18%
4	11%
5 or more	29%

To what degree do you agree (or disagree) with the statement, "I *really* like my group."

Strongly disagree	.4%
Somewhat disagree	.3%
Neutral	11%
Somewhat agree	34%
Strongly agree	48%

Survey #5:
Participants Survey

This survey was roughly the same as the original one, with one big exception. I wanted to see how participants' views of things differed from perceptions of the teachers. Following are the answers I used in the book.

How would you rate your teacher's strength in the following areas:

TEACHING ABILITY

    1 star 1.1%

    2 stars 4.3%

    3 stars 15.0%

    4 stars 30.2%

    5 stars 49.4%

PEOPLE SKILLS

    1 star 1.1%

    2 stars 3.2%

    3 stars 16.9%

    4 stars 27.1%

    5 stars 51.7%

SPIRITUAL VIBRANCY

    1 star 1.4%

    2 stars 6.1%

    3 stars 10.0%

    4 stars 28.6%

    5 stars 53.9%

ORGANIZATIONAL SKILL

    1 star 2.3%

    2 stars 7.5%

    3 stars 17.5%

    4 stars 28.3%

    5 stars 44.4%

Quick Survey

This was a very short follow-up survey, which focused on a couple of very specific issues.

When was the last time you had guests into your home for dinner or dessert?

Within the last month. 57%

Within the last three months 15%

Within the last year 14%

Can't remember the last time 14%

Which statement is the most accurate about your church?

My pastor regularly and enthus-
astically promotes group life or
Sunday school from the
pulpit. 48%

My pastor occasionally mentions
group life or Sunday school
from the pulpit. 37%

My pastor never or almost never
mentions Sunday school or
group life from the pulpit. 15%

Chapter 2:
Four Things That Matter...Some

1. Tom Rath, *Strengths Finder 2.0* (Gallup Press, 2007), p. 7.
2. Rath, p. 7.
3. Rath, p. iii.

Section Two: Introduction

1. Aletha Hinthorn, "Multiply Your Prayer Power," Church of God (Holiness), April 2009, http://www.cogh.net/multiply-your-prayer-power

Chapter 3:
The Group That Parties Together Grows Together

1. Richard T. Ritenbaugh, "Sermon: Hospitality," Church of the Great God, July 2007, http://cgg.org/index.cfm/fuseaction/Audio.details/ID/1975/Hospitality.htm
2. Robert B. Cialdini, *Influence: The Psychology of Persuasion* (New York: Morrow, 1993).
3. Robert D. Putnam, *Bowling Alone* (New York: Simon & Schuster, 2001), p. 183. Used by permission.
4. Lisa F. Berkman and S. Leonard Syme, "Social Networks, Host Resistance, and Mortality: A Nine-year Follow-up Study of Alameda County Residents," *American Journal of Epidemiology*, 109: 2, p. 186, http://aje.oxfordjournals.org/content/abstract/109/2/186
5. John Ortberg, "The Power of Belonging," March 2008, http://mppc.org/sites/default/files/transcripts/080316_jortberg.pdf
6. Jane E. Brody, "A Cold Fact: High Stress Can Make You Sick," *The New York Times*, May 12, 1998, http://www.nytimes.com/specials/women/warchive/980512_940.html
7. Martin E.P. Seligman, *Authentic Happiness* (New York: Free Press, 2002), 117.

Chapter 4:
Go Team!

1. John C. Maxwell, *The 21 Irrefutable Laws of Leadership* (Nashville: Thomas Nelson, 1998).

Chapter 5:
Like Your Group—and Show It

1. Tim Sanders, *The Likeability Factor* (New York: Three Rivers Press, 2005, 2006) p. 30-31.
2. John Ortberg, "Goodness," http://mppc.org/sites/default/files/transcripts/040725_jortberg_tr.pdf

Chapter 6:
Spiritual Vibrancy—What It Is and How to Get It

1. Misty Bernall, *She Said Yes* (Nashville: Word Publishing, 1999).

Chapter 7:
You Gotta Have Faith

1. Brian Tracy, *Goals!* (San Francisco: Berrett-Koehler, 2003), p. 70.
2. Tom Rath and Barry Conchie, *Strengths Based Leadership* (New York: Gallup Press, 2008), p. 15-16.
3. Everett M. Rogers, *Diffusion of Innovations* (New York: Free Press, 2003), p. 31-34.
4. Rogers, p. 31-34.
5. Kerry Patterson, *Influencer: The Power to Change Anything* (New York: McGraw Hill, 2008), p. 148.

Chapter 8:
Pastors, Lead the Way!

1. Allan Taylor, *Sunday School in HD* (Nashville: B&H Books, 2009), p. 134.
2. Larry Osborne, *Sticky Church* (Grand Rapids, MI: Zondervan, 2008).
3. Nelson Searcy and Kerrick Thomas, *Activate* (Ventura, CA: Regal, 2008) p. 59.
4. Steve Parr, "Georgia's Fastest Growing Sunday Schools," Sunday School/Open Group Ministries and Research Services of the Georgia Baptist Convention,
5. Osborne, *Sticky Church*, p. 136-137.
6. Nelson Searcy, *Activate*, p. 187.
7. Adrian Gostick and Chester Elton, *The Carrot Principle* (New York: Free Press, 2007) p. 7.

Chapter 9:
Leaders, Go Forth: A 10-Step Strategy

1. David Murrow, *Why Men Hate Going to Church* (Nashville: Thomas Nelson, 2004).
2. Jim Collins and Jerry Porras, *Built to Last* (New York: HarperBusiness, 2004).
3. Gary Thomas, *Sacred Pathways* (Grand Rapids: Zondervan, 2010).